Vegetarian PIZZA

C O O K B O O K

Vegetarian PIZZA
COOKBOOK

INNOVATIVE RECIPES FOR MOUTH-WATERING PIZZAS WITH MEAT-FREE TOPPINGS

MAUREEN KELLER

CHARTWELL
BOOKS, INC.

A QUINTET BOOK

Published by Chartwell Books
A Division of Book Sales, Inc.
114, Northfield Avenue
Edison, New Jersey 08837

This edition produced for sale in the U.S.A., its
territories and dependencies only.

ISBN 0-7858-0552-4

This book was designed and produced by
Quintet Publishing Limited
6 Blundell Street
London N7 9BH

Creative Director: Richard Dewing
Designer: Jill Coote
Senior Editor: Laura Sandelson
Editor: Maggi McCormick
Photographer: Andrew Whittuck

Typeset in Great Britain by
Central Southern Typesetters, Eastbourne
Manufactured in Singapore by
Bright Arts (Pte) Ltd
Printed in Singapore by
Star Standard Industries (Pte) Ltd

Acknowledgements
The Publishers would like to thank *The Red Pepper*,
Formosa Street, London W9, for generously
allowing the photographing of their pizza chef,
Nino Pasquale, at work.

CONTENTS

INTRODUCTION

Hardly known outside Italy before the turn of the century, pizza
is one of the most popular foods in the United States. So huge is
the pizza phenomenon, it may soon replace the hamburger as
America's favorite food.

Americans eat approximately 100 acres of pizza each day, according to the National Association of Pizza Operators. It's a $40 billion-a-year industry with more than 58,000 pizzerias in the United States, and more opening up all the time. Pizzerias represent approximately 17 percent of total restaurants in the United States and pizza restaurant growth outpaces overall restaurant growth. *Parade Magazine* estimates that 94 percent of the American population eats pizza.

Why is pizza so popular? Maybe because it's nutritious – the *Encyclopedia of Food and Nutrition* describes pizza as a "reasonably well-balanced" meal. Maybe because it's fun – we eat it with our hands. Or possibly, we like it because it's easy – it's the number one food delivery item. Or, it could just be that the popularity of pizza is because of its taste. Pizza, quite simply, is delicious. Guaranteed satisfaction.

Although once a favorite meal only in Italy, today pizza is turning up everywhere.

BELOW Pizza is not only fun to eat but is nutritious, easy to cook, and inexpensive.

ABOVE A great pizza depends on fresh vegetables and other good quality ingredients.

Whether you're in Switzerland, Costa Rica, Japan, or China, you can find a restaurant or a cafe baking the popular pies. Toppings vary to reflect regional preferences. In Japan, for example, eel and squid are favorite toppings; in Pakistan it's curry. Russia is big on red herring, while Australians enjoy shrimp and pineapple. In the U.S., the favorite topping is pepperoni, but vegetarian toppings are also popular. In 1994, Americans topped their pizzas with 1.4 million pounds of mushrooms, 59.3 million pounds of green peppers, and 2.7 million cases of olives.

If one defines pizza as a flat piece of bread with toppings, then pizza probably originated in prehistoric times, not long after the discovery of fire. It's not hard to imagine cave men and women sitting around the campfire enjoying such treats. Flat bread is easily cooked on hot stones.

And it wouldn't have taken long to think of spreading something on top.

But the credit for the modern pizza is given to the citizens of Naples, Italy. As the story goes, the women of the town used to bake their bread in large communal ovens. As they sat around chatting and waiting, they got hungry. Someone pinched off some of the dough, flattened it, cooked it quickly in the hot ovens, topped it with herbs and olive oil, and the modern pizza was born.

The tomato wasn't an early topping for pizza because Europeans had never seen one until they started exploring South America. The tomato was a fruit that grew in the foothills of the Andes Mountains in the area that today covers parts of Peru, Ecuador, and Bolivia. Explorers took tomato seeds back to Spain in the 16th century. Around 1522, the tomato showed up in Naples, but it took another two hundred years for it to top a pizza. At first, the tomato was thought to be pretty but poisonous and was used strictly for ornamentation. But by the early 1700s, tomatoes had taken their place of honor in Italian cooking. The first recipe for tomato sauce was published in Rome in 1705, and it wasn't long before it was, at least occasionally, topping pizza. By the mid-1800s, tomatoes had become an almost essential topping for the pies. Last year, 3.7 billion pounds of tomatoes were used on pizza in the U.S. alone.

In 1889 another advance in pizza progress occurred: mozzarella cheese was added. When the Queen of Italy, Margherita Teresa Giovanni, visited Naples, she wanted to sample the popular local dish, pizza. Chef Raffele Esposito was asked to create one in her honor. He created three new pizzas for her and she chose as her favorite one topped with tomato sauce, basil and mozzarella. It was delicious *and* it also displayed the colors of the Italian flag. The red, white, and green pizza became known as margherita pizza and is still found today on the menus of many Italian eateries. And, of course, mozzarella went on to become a favorite pizza topping.

LEFT Using well-flavored ingredients such as sun-dried tomatoes elevates the humble pizza from the ordinary to the extraordinary.

ABOVE The authentic texture and smoky flavor of pizzas is usually as a result of baking in a wood-burning oven.

True mozzarella cheese, as it was made in the days of Queen Margherita, is made from the milk of water buffalos. It is a soft-ripening cheese that improves with age, but which lasts only five to six weeks.

Mozzarella made in the U.S., however, is made from cow's milk. Buffalo mozzarella can be found in specialty cheese shops, but most is made with a combination of cow and water buffalo milk. Today, mozzarella cheese represents 30 percent of the total cheese produced in the U.S., according to the *Cheese Market News*. U.S. production of Italian cheeses, such as mozzarella, provolone, ricotta, Romano and Parmesan, more than doubled between 1980 and 1992, from 688.6 million pounds per year to nearly two billion pounds. This growth was due in no small part to the increasing popularity of pizza. Last year, Americans consumed 1.9 billion pounds of mozzarella on their pizzas.

Pizza first came to the U.S. with Italian immigrants who brought it with them to Chicago and New York. It could be found in ethnic pockets of those cities, but was not widely popular. The first true pizzeria in America opened in 1905 on Spring Street in New York. Pizza's popularity didn't soar until after World War II. U.S. servicemen stationed in Europe discovered pizza and returned home after the war raving about it. Today, pizza is as much an American dish as the hamburger.

Although pizza was created in Italy, it has evolved in the U.S. There are thin crusts and deep-dish crusts, Chicago pizza, New York pizza, and California pizza. And it's Americans who can be credited with taking the pizza worldwide. Pizza Hut, which sells the most pizzas in the world, has more then 500,000 franchises in 69 countries.

Pizza has become so popular in America that it permeates the culture. It has been immortalized in song – *That's Amore*; in films – *Mystic Pizza*; and in business – Licorice Pizza (a chain of music stores). The local library in my city has an entire category called "pizza fiction" which lists more than 75 books and records that immortalize the pie. Americans also use pizza to reach for their 15 minutes of fame. In 1991 in Havana, Florida, Lorenzo Amato and Louis Piancone made the largest pizza ever baked in the U.S. It was 10,057 square feet and measured 140 feet across. It weighed 44,457 pounds and consisted of 18,174 pounds of flour, 8,103 pounds of water, 6,445 pounds of sauce, 9,375 pounds of cheese, and 2,387 pounds of pepperoni. (The largest pizza in the world – 11,816 square feet – was baked in Norwood, Johannesburg, South Africa, in 1990.)

Pizza has made inroads into the culture of other non-Italian countries as well. Domino's Pizza reports that Christmas Eve is one of its highest grossing days in Japan because it has become a tradition to order in for pizza that night. In Ireland, pizza sales peak during St. Patrick's Day festivities.

Pizza has become such a big business that there is a trade association for people who sell it – the National Association of Pizza Operators – and a magazine, *Pizza Today*, which includes topics such as marketing to children, regional sauces and exotic vegetables. The trade association sponsors an annual Pizza Expo for those in the business. It includes the crowd-pleasing "Pizzaahlympics," a series of pizza-tossing events that test the skills of pizza makers from around the world.

One reason pizza is so popular must be the ease with which it can be purchased and eaten. Pizza is the quintessential take-out food, having been sold on the streets of Naples. It's sold frozen in the supermarket. You can buy it by the slice or by the pie. Or you can purchase prepacked ingredients and assemble it at home. There are prebaked crusts or dough in a can that you bake yourself. You can buy premade sauce and prepackaged, shredded cheese. But the best pizza, of course, is the one that you make from scratch. It is not only the tastiest, it's also the most fun.

BELOW The enduring popularity of pizzas is undoubtedly them being the number one fast food in many countries around the world.

PIZZA FOR KIDS

Because pizza is so much fun to make, it's the perfect meal to prepare with children. Kids between the ages of 3 and 11 prefer pizza over all other foods for lunch and dinner, according to a Gallup Poll. To kids, pounding and kneading the dough is a lot like playing. Watching the dough rise is fascinating and rewarding, and pizza dough can be fashioned into all sorts of shapes and decorated creatively. Children can customize each pie and include foods they like, and eliminate those they don't. They can make faces, flowers, animals, or whatever their imaginations come up with. It's almost impossible to fail. And because pizza is also nutritious, it's healthier than making dessert.

MAKING DOUGH

Good pizza begins with good dough. It may take a little practice, but it isn't difficult to make a good crust. If you have a bread-making machine, making crust is easy. But special equipment is not necessary.

RIGHT The ingredients for good dough are extremely basic: yeast, oil, flour, water, and salt.

RIGHT A strong pair of hands is needed to make the dough smooth and elastic.

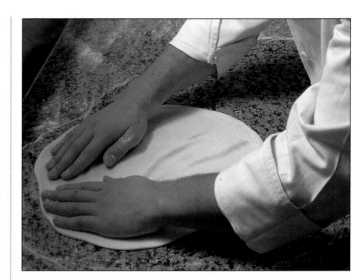

ABOVE Professional pizza chefs are able to shape the dough into a perfect round using only their hands.

Just a bowl, a good set of hands, and the ingredients are all you need.

Here are a few tips. Make sure the yeast you use is fresh (check the expiration date on the package). Store yeast in the refrigerator, but bring it to room temperature before using. When you add warm liquid to activate the yeast, remember that heat kills. If the liquid is too hot, the yeast will be killed and the dough won't rise. The ideal temperature for the warm liquid is 100° to 115°.

Once the flour and other ingredients have been added, the dough will be sticky. But as you knead it, the dough picks up flour from your hands, which you dust with flour, and from the board on which you are working and eventually becomes smooth and elastic. Because different batches of flour have different moisture content, the flour-to-liquid ratio needed to reach the proper consistency varies. Follow the recipes given, but add the liquid a little at a time, adding more or less to reach the consistency desired. But remember, too much flour results in a baked crust that's hard. Cooking the pizza too long also results in a hard crust. It may take a bit of experimenting to attain the perfect crust. Ovens vary in heat distribution and temperature and cooks vary in how they mix and roll out the dough.

Pizza dough keeps wonderfully in the freezer, so when you bake, make a double or triple batch and save it to use later. After the dough rises, divide it into the sizes you need and pat the dough into flattened balls. Freeze them in freezer bags. Thaw them in the refrigerator as needed and then roll them out and top. Keep frozen dough on hand and you can throw a quick, delicious meal together in no time.

Making your own dough is the fun part of making a pizza, but if you aren't so inclined, there are many products in the supermarket. Any packaged biscuit dough – whether buttermilk, crescent roll, or corn bread – makes a quick crust. Just roll it out in one piece on a pizza pan. You can also, of course, buy prepacked dough to roll out yourself, or prebaked crusts that are ready to top and reheat.

SPECIAL EQUIPMENT

You can bake a good pizza in any pizza pan. But crusts can be improved with the aid of special equipment. Ceramic pizza stones placed in your oven while it preheats create a piping hot surface on which to bake the pizza. This method produces the crisp brown crusts one gets from pizzas baked in commercial ovens. Quarry tiles also can be used. If you bake on stone or tiles, you will need a long-handled wooden board, called a peel, to move the pizza, first onto the tile, and when done, to remove it. Another option is to bake pizza on a pizza screen or in a perforated pan. Both allow air to circulate during the baking process to prevent soggy or greasy crusts.

FINAL THOUGHTS

While meat toppings remain the most popular, non-meat pizza is the perfect meal for a vegetarian. Whether you only avoid meat or are a true vegan, the flat pizza pie is the perfect base for a variety of delicious meals. Pizza has become so versatile it can be served as an appetizer, a snack, a side dish, a main course, or a dessert. It can be made in individual-sized portions or in pies big enough for a party. This cookbook offers a sampling of the variety of dishes that can be served as pizza. Use it as inspiration. Let your vegetarian pizza adventure begin.

LEFT The professional way to achieve the correct thickness of pizza base is to hurl it in the air.

BASIC DOUGH RECIPES

▚▚▚▚▚

BASIC PIZZA DOUGH

MAKES TWO 12-INCH REGULAR-CRUST PIZZAS
OR ONE DOUBLE-CRUST PIZZA

Basic pizza dough goes well with just about any topping you like.
It is the classic Italian crust.

1 package active dry yeast
1 cup warm water
2½ cups unbleached white flour
2 tbsp olive oil
½ tsp salt

1 In a large bowl, combine the yeast, warm water, and 1½ cups of the flour. Mix well to blend. Add the oil, salt, and remaining flour and stir until the dough sticks together.

2 Place the dough on a lightly floured surface. Dust your hands with flour and knead the dough until it is smooth and elastic, about five minutes. If the dough gets sticky, sprinkle it with a little flour.

1

2

3

3 Roll the dough into a ball and place it in a lightly oiled bowl. Cover the bowl with a dishtowel and set in a warm, but not hot, place to rise until doubled in volume, about one hour.

4 When the dough has risen, roll it into a ball to make one 12-inch regular crust pizza or divide it in two balls to make two thin-crust 12-inch pizzas. Before rolling out and topping the pizza, allow the dough to rest for 20 minutes.

5 When ready to bake, place dough in center of lightly oiled pan. Roll outward toward the edges with the palm of your hand until the dough fills the pan evenly.

4

5

WHOLE WHEAT PIZZA DOUGH

Whole wheat flour adds robust flavor to the dough, but this
recipe also calls for regular flour. On its own, whole wheat flour is
too heavy to make a proper crust. It, too, goes well
with most toppings.

1 package active dry yeast
1 cup warm water
1¼ cups unbleached white flour
2 tbsp olive oil
½ tsp salt
1 cup whole wheat flour

❖ In a large bowl, combine the yeast, warm
water, and white flour. Mix well to blend.
Add the oil, salt, and whole wheat flour and
stir until the dough sticks together. Place
the dough on a lightly floured surface.
Dust your hands with flour and then knead
the dough until it is smooth and elastic,
about five minutes. If the dough gets sticky,
sprinkle it with a little more flour.

❖ Roll the dough into a ball and place it in
a lightly oiled bowl. Cover the bowl with a
dishtowel and set in a warm, but not hot,
place to rise until doubled in volume, about
one hour.

❖ When the dough has risen, roll it into a
ball to make one 12-inch regular crust
pizza or divide it in two balls to make two
thin-crust 12-inch pizzas. Before rolling
out and topping the pizza, allow the dough
to rest for 20 minutes.

❖ When ready to bake, place dough in
center of lightly oiled pan. Roll outward
toward the edges with the palm of your
hand until the dough fills the pan evenly.

CORN BREAD PIZZA DOUGH

MAKES ONE REGULAR 12-INCH PIZZA

Corn bread goes well with many toppings, most notably those with tomato-based sauces such as Creole, jambalaya, or Mexican-style toppings. It also goes well with cheeses.

1 cup warm water

1 package active dry yeast

1½ cups unbleached white flour

¾ cup yellow corn meal

¼ tsp salt

1 tsp sugar

2 tbsp corn oil

◆ In a large bowl, combine the warm water, yeast, 1 cup of white flour, and ¼ cup of corn meal. Stir to mix thoroughly. Add the remaining ingredients, stirring with a wooden spoon until mixed. Place the dough on a floured surface. Dust your hands with white flour and knead the dough for five minutes, dusting with additional white flour if necessary to keep it from sticking. Dough should be smooth and elastic.

◆ Place the dough in a clean bowl, cover with cloth, and set in a warm place to rise for about one hour or until doubled in size.

◆ When dough is ready, roll into a ball and set aside to rest for 20 minutes before topping and baking.

WHOLE WHEAT CHEESE PIZZA DOUGH

MAKES TWO 12-INCH REGULAR CRUST PIZZAS
OR ONE DOUBLE-CRUST PIZZA

Parmesan cheese adds a sharpness to the crust. Other types of grated hard cheese can be substituted for the Parmesan, but soft cheeses melt and stick to the pan.

1 package active dry yeast

1 cup warm water

1¼ cups unbleached white flour

4 tsp olive oil

½ tsp salt

¼ cup grated Parmesan cheese

1 cup whole wheat flour

◆ Follow instructions as for Whole Wheat Pizza Dough (see page 16), but add the Parmesan cheese to the oil and salt which will then be added to the yeast mixture.

JALAPEÑO-TOMATO PIZZA DOUGH

⬛⬜⬛⬜⬛⬜⬛

MAKES TWO 12-INCH REGULAR CRUST PIZZAS
OR ONE DOUBLE-CRUST PIZZA

This dough is hot and colorful, and makes a dramatic presentation. It comes out red with bright green specks. Make sure to mince the peppers very finely. Good toppings for this crust include corn and tomatoes.

1 package active dry yeast

1 cup tomato or vegetable juice

2 jalapeño peppers, seeded and diced very finely (about 2 tbsp)

2½ cups unbleached white flour

2 tbsp olive oil

½ tsp salt

◈ In a large bowl, combine the yeast, juice, jalapeño peppers, and 1½ cups of flour. Mix well to blend. Add the oil, salt, and remaining flour and stir until the dough sticks together. Place the dough on a lightly floured surface. Dust your hands with flour and knead the dough until it is smooth and elastic, about five minutes. If the dough gets sticky, sprinkle it with a little more flour.

◈ Roll the dough into a ball and place it in a lightly oiled bowl. Cover the bowl with a dishtowel and set in a warm, but not hot, place to rise until doubled in volume, about one hour.

◈ When the dough has risen, roll it into a ball to make one 12-inch regular crust pizza or divide it into two balls to make two thin-crust 12-inch pizzas. Before rolling out and topping the pizza, allow the dough to rest for 20 minutes.

◈ When ready to bake, place dough in center of lightly oiled pan. Roll outward toward the edges with the palm of your hand until the dough fills the pan evenly.

⬛⬜⬛⬜⬛⬜⬛

◄ Clockwise
from left:
Jalapeño —
Tomato Pizza
Dough, Whole
Wheat Cheese
Pizza Dough,
and Corn
Bread Pizza
Dough.

GARLIC DILL PIZZA DOUGH

MAKES TWO 12-INCH REGULAR CRUST PIZZAS
OR ONE DOUBLE-CRUST PIZZA

The more garlic you add to this recipe, the more it tastes like garlic bread. Any topping that can be complemented by garlic goes well on this crust. It is even good just topped with cheese.

1 package active dry yeast
1 cup warm water
1 tsp dried dill
2 cloves garlic (or more), minced
2½ cups unbleached white flour
2 tbsp olive oil
½ tsp salt

◆ In a large bowl, combine the yeast, warm water, dill, garlic, and 1½ cups of the flour. Mix well to blend. Add the oil, salt, and remaining flour and stir until the dough sticks together. Place the dough on a lightly floured surface. Dust your hands with flour and knead the dough until it is smooth and elastic, about five minutes. If the dough gets sticky, sprinkle it with a little flour.

◆ Roll the dough into a ball and place it in a lightly oiled bowl. Cover the bowl with a dishtowel and set in a warm, but not hot, place to rise until doubled in volume, about one hour.

◆ When the dough has risen, roll it into a ball to make one 12-inch regular crust pizza or divide it in two balls to make two thin-crust 12-inch pizzas. Before rolling out and topping the pizza, allow the dough to rest for 20 minutes.

◆ When ready to bake, place dough in center of lightly oiled pan. Roll outward toward the edges with the palm of your hand until the dough fills the pan evenly.

CHINESE PIZZA DOUGH

MAKES TWO 12-INCH REGULAR CRUST PIZZAS
OR ONE DOUBLE-CRUST PIZZA

Sesame seeds and soy sauce give this dough an Oriental flavor. It is good with any stir-fry, Chinese, or Thai-style topping.

1 package active dry yeast
1 cup warm water
1½ cups unbleached white flour
4 tsp olive oil

½ tsp salt
2 tbsp sesame seeds
1 tbsp soy sauce
1 cup whole wheat flour

In a large bowl, combine the yeast, warm water, and white flour. Mix well to blend. Add the oil, salt, sesame seeds, and soy sauce and mix thoroughly. Add the whole wheat flour and stir until the dough sticks together. Place the dough on a flat surface lightly dusted with white flour. Dust your hands with white flour and then knead the dough until it is smooth and elastic, about five minutes. If the dough gets sticky, sprinkle it with a little more flour.

Roll the dough into a ball and place it in a lightly oiled bowl. Cover the bowl with a dishtowel and set in a warm, but not hot, place to rise until doubled in volume, about one hour.

When the dough has risen, roll it into a ball to make one 12-inch regular crust pizza or divide it in two balls to make two thin-crust 12-inch pizzas. Before rolling out and topping the pizza, allow the dough to rest for 20 minutes.

When ready to bake, place dough in center of lightly oiled pan. Roll outward toward the edges with the palm of your hand until the dough fills the pan evenly.

▲ *Above* Garlic Dill Pizza Dough. *Below* Chinese Pizza Dough.

STOVE-TOP NO-YEAST CRUST

MAKES TWO 9-INCH REGULAR CRUSTS

If you're in a hurry and don't have time to make a traditional pizza dough, this crust, made with baking powder instead of yeast, is a fine substitute. It is fried on top of the stove in just a few minutes and can be topped with anything you want.

1 cup whole wheat flour
1 cup white flour
½ tsp salt
2 tsp baking powder
2 tbsp olive oil
6–8 tbsp cold water

◆ Mix flours, salt, and baking powder thoroughly. Add oil. Mix in the water a little at a time until dough holds together well but is not sticky. Knead for a few minutes and then allow to rest for five minutes before cooking.

◆ Divide the dough in half. Roll each half into a round the size of your skillet (probably 9 inches). Use a pizza cutter to round off the edges so that it is a nice circle. Heat 1 tbsp oil and fry until browned, about five minutes on the first side, and three on the second. Remove from the pan and cook the second pizza.

◆ Top each pizza with desired topping and broil for a few minutes until topping is heated and any cheese melted.

RYE BREAD PIZZA DOUGH

MAKES TWO 12-INCH REGULAR CRUST PIZZAS
OR ONE DOUBLE-CRUST PIZZA

Rye flour adds a special taste and texture to a dough. For variation, add caraway seeds, as is done with rye bread. Vegetable and cheese toppings go well with this crust.

1 package active dry yeast
1 cup warm water
1¼ cups unbleached white flour
4 tsp olive oil

½ tsp salt
1 tbsp maple syrup
1 cup rye flour

In a large bowl, combine the yeast, warm water, and white flour. Mix well to blend. Add the oil, salt, maple syrup, and rye flour and stir until the dough sticks together. Place the dough on a lightly floured surface. Dust your hands with flour and then knead the dough until it is smooth and elastic, about five minutes. If the dough gets sticky, sprinkle more flour.

Roll out the dough into a ball and place it in a lightly oiled bowl. Cover the bowl with a dishtowel and set in a warm, but not hot, place to rise until double in volume, about one hour.

When the dough has risen, roll it into a ball to make one 12-inch regular crust pizza or divide it in two balls to make two thin-crust 12-inch pizzas. Before rolling out and topping the pizza, allow the dough to rest for 20 minutes.

When ready to bake, place dough in center of lightly oiled pan. Roll outward toward the edges with the palm of your hand until the dough fills the pan evenly.

CHOCOLATE DESSERT CRUST

MAKES ONE REGULAR 12-INCH CRUST

This is a very sweet crust that goes well with light fruit concoctions on top. It could even be used as the basis for an ice-cream pizza.

2 oz unsweetened chocolate
½ cup butter, softened to room temperature
1 cup sugar
1 egg, beaten
1 tsp vanilla extract
1½ tsp baking powder
¼ tsp salt
1½ cups all-purpose flour

Preheat oven to 400°.

Melt the unsweetened chocolate in the top half of a double boiler. Cool.

In a bowl, cream together the softened butter and sugar. When well mixed, stir in the egg and vanilla. Then add the baking powder, salt, cooled chocolate, and flour and mix thoroughly. Cover and place in the freezer for 45 minutes to stiffen the dough.

Coat the pizza pan with vegetable spray and place the stiffened dough in the center. Spread the dough with your hands until it covers the pan evenly. Use a glass, rolling it on its side over the dough to smooth it out if necessary.

Bake at 400° for 10 minutes. Allow to cool before topping.

DESSERT PIZZA CRUST

MAKES ONE REGULAR 12-INCH DESSERT CRUST

A sweet dough-like a sugar cookie, makes this dessert crust good topped with any fruit mixture.

¾ cup vegetable oil

1 cup sugar

2 eggs

1 tsp vanilla extract

1½ tsp baking powder

¼ tsp salt

2½ cups all-purpose flour

◆ Preheat oven to 375°.

◆ In a large bowl, combine the oil and sugar, stirring until mixed thoroughly. Beat in the eggs and vanilla. Finally, add the baking powder, salt, and flour and stir until thoroughly mixed. Refrigerate the dough for 15 minutes to stiffen it.

◆ Spray vegetable oil on a 12-inch round pizza pan. Place the refrigerated dough in the middle and then begin working it out toward the edges with your ands until the dough fills the pan evenly. Bake for 15 minutes. Cool completely before topping.

GINGERBREAD CRUST

MAKES ONE REGULAR 12-INCH CRUST

If it goes with gingerbread, it will taste good on this crust. Try apples and dried fruit mixtures with whipping cream sauces.

¼ cup butter

¼ cup sugar

1 egg

1 tsp baking powder

½ tsp cinnamon

½ tsp ginger

¼ tsp salt

1¾ cup flour

2 tbsp unsulfured molasses

1 tbsp honey

◆ Preheat oven to 350°.

◆ Cream the butter and sugar together. Beat in the egg. Add the baking powder, spices, and salt. Add the flour, molasses, and honey, stirring to mix thoroughly. Refrigerate the dough for about 15 minutes to stiffen it.

◆ Coat a pizza pan with cooking spray. Place dough in the middle and then work it out to the edges so that it covers the pan evenly. If necessary, use the side of a glass (refrigerate the glass along with the dough). Bake for 15 minutes. Cool before adding toppings.

▶ *Top* Chocolate Dessert Crust, *center* Dessert Pizza Crust, and *bottom* Gingerbread Crust.

PIZZAS
WITH
TOMATOES

DEEP-DISH CREOLE PIZZA

MAKES ONE 9 x 13-INCH DEEP-DISH PIZZA

Creole dishes tend to be spicy tomato and vegetable mixtures, and this pizza is no exception. You can try using fresh okra if it is available. Boil the whole fresh okra until tender. Then chop it to use in this recipe.

1 batch Basic or Whole Wheat Pizza Dough
  (see page 14 or 16)
2 14½-oz cans stewed tomatoes
1 tsp oregano
1 tsp thyme
½ tsp basil
½ tsp cayenne pepper
2 cloves garlic, minced
2 stalks celery, chopped
1 small onion, chopped
2 cups cut frozen okra, thawed

◆ Preheat oven to 500°.
◆ Place the dough in the center of a lightly oiled 13 x 9 x 2-inch pan. Using your fingers, gently spread the dough until it covers the bottom of the pan evenly and goes halfway up the sides.
◆ Put the stewed tomatoes into a colander and drain and discard the liquid but retain the thick sauce. Cut the tomatoes into fourths. Place the tomatoes and sauce in a bowl. Add the spices and garlic. Chop the celery and onions into small pieces and add them to the bowl. Finally, add the okra and stir gently to mix.
◆ To assemble, spread the tomato and okra mixture onto the pizza dough and bake for 20 minutes.

PIZZA SAUCE

MAKES ABOUT 2¾ CUPS SAUCE

Puréed tomatoes have the perfect consistency for pizza sauce. If you make extra sauce and freeze it, you'll always have some on hand.

1 28-oz can puréed tomatoes
1 bay leaf
1 tsp oregano
1 tsp basil
1 tsp thyme
½ tsp marjoram

◆ Place ingredients in a pan and bring to a boil. Reduce heat, cover loosely to keep from spattering, and simmer for 30 minutes, stirring occasionally.

▲ Deep-dish Creole Pizza.

BOUNTIFUL HARVEST PIZZA

MAKES ONE 12-INCH DOUBLE-CRUST PIZZA

This is a basic vegetarian pizza with a variety of colors and textures. Experiment by adding whichever of your favorite vegetables are in season.

1 batch Whole Wheat Pizza Dough
 (see page 16)
⅔ cup Pizza Sauce (see page 28)
1 small onion, chopped
½ green pepper, chopped
½ red bell pepper, chopped
½ cup mushrooms, sliced
¾ cup broccoli flowerets
½ cup shredded mozzarella cheese
½ cup grated Romano cheese

◆ Preheat oven to 500°.
◆ Spread the pizza sauce onto the pizza dough, leaving a ½-inch edge. Spread the chopped onions, green and red peppers, sliced mushrooms, and broccoli flowerets over the sauce. Finish with the mozzarella and then the Romano cheese. Bake for 10 minutes.

PIZZA WITH PORTABELLA MUSHROOMS

MAKES ONE 12-INCH DOUBLE-CRUST PIZZA

Some vegetarians consider the large portabella mushroom a good substitute for meat. Basted and cooked in a very hot oven, they can taste almost like a steak.

1 batch Whole Wheat Cheese Pizza Dough
 (see page 17)
6 cloves garlic, unpeeled
¾ cup Pizza Sauce (see page 28)
1 medium onion, chopped
½ cup mozzarella cheese
½ cup Monterey Jack
6 oz portabella mushrooms
3–4 tbsp olive oil
1 tbsp parsley flakes

◆ Preheat oven to 500°.
◆ Boil the unpeeled garlic in water for about 20 minutes. When cool enough to touch, squeeze one end and the cooked mushy garlic should pop out.
◆ Spread the garlic around the pizza dough. Top with the pizza sauce. Sprinkle the chopped onions over the sauce. Spread the mozzarella and then the jack cheese. Slice the mushrooms into ¼-inch thick pieces. Brush liberally with the oil. Arrange on top of the cheese and finally sprinkle on the parsley flakes.
◆ Bake for 10 minutes.

◀ Left
Bountiful
Harvest Pizza.

PIZZA WITH CARAMELIZED ONIONS

MAKES ONE 12-INCH DOUBLE-CRUST PIZZA

Caramelized onions are cooked slowly in oil until they are golden
brown and very soft. They have a wonderful flavor that goes well
on a pizza. Make them ahead of time and store them in the
refrigerator until ready to use.

1 batch Basic or Whole Wheat Pizza Dough
  (see page 14 or 16)
2 large onions
3 tbsp olive oil
½ tsp salt
2 tsp red wine vinegar
¾ cup Pizza Sauce (see page 28)
¾ cup grated fontina cheese

◆ Preheat the oven to 500°.

◆ Slice both ends off the onions but do not peel. Cut the onions in quarters. Place them skin side down in a roasting pan. Liberally brush each onion with 1 tablespoon of the oil and sprinkle with salt. Cover the pan with foil and bake for 30 minutes. After 30 minutes, remove the foil and brush the onion with the remaining oil. Sprinkle with vinegar. Turn onion quarters on one side and return to the oven for one hour. Occasionally turn the onions and baste with the oil from the pan. When done, allow to cool or store in refrigerator for later use.

◆ When ready to reassemble the pizza, slice onion quarters into strips. Spread the pizza sauce over the pizza dough. Spread sliced onion over the sauce and top with cheese. Bake for 10 minutes.

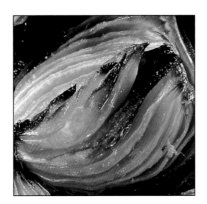

SUN-DRIED TOMATOES AND MOZZARELLA PIZZA

MAKES ONE 12-INCH DOUBLE-CRUST PIZZA

This pizza is simple to make, yet elegant enough for a party!
For best results, allow the tomatoes to marinate overnight in
the refrigerator.

1 batch Basic Pizza Dough (see page 14)

3 oz sun-dried tomatoes

3 tbsp extra virgin olive oil

4 cloves garlic, crushed

4 oz round mozzarella cheese, sliced

½ tsp dried basil

◆ Chop the sun-dried tomatoes into bite-sized pieces. Then put the tomatoes, olive oil, and garlic in a container and marinate at room temperature for 30 minutes or overnight in the refrigerator. Slice the mozzarella into thin rounds.

◄ *Left* Sun-Dried Tomatoes and Mozzarella Pizza.

◆ Preheat oven to 500°. Bake the dough for five minutes and remove from oven.

◆ To assemble the pizza, place the mozzarella rounds on the prebaked crust, leaving room between each slice. Spread the sun-dried tomato mixture on top of the cheese, pouring the olive oil on as well. Sprinkle with dried basil. Bake for four or five minutes or until tomatoes begin to brown.

EGGPLANT PARMESAN PIZZA

MAKES ONE 12-INCH DOUBLE-CRUST PIZZA

Eggplant is a wonderfully versatile vegetable, worth growing in a backyard garden. Soaking the sliced eggplant in salted water before cooking eliminates any bitterness.

1 batch Whole Wheat Pizza Dough
  (see page 16)
1 medium eggplant
water
1 tbsp salt
¾ cup Pizza Sauce (see page 28)
3 oz mozzarella cheese, sliced
1 tbsp olive oil
¼ cup grated Parmesan cheese
2 tsp parsley

◆ Preheat oven to 500°. Bake the crust for five minutes and remove from oven.

◆ Peel the eggplant and slice into thin rounds for quick cooking. Place the eggplant in a bowl of water with the tablespoon of salt and soak for 20 minutes. You may need to weight the eggplant down with a glass jar. After soaking, rinse thoroughly and squeeze it between paper towels to remove moisture.

◆ To assemble pizza, spread the pizza sauce on the prebaked crust, leaving a ½-inch edge. Next, arrange the mozzarella slices over the sauce. Top them with eggplant slices. Sprinkle the olive oil over the eggplant. Spread the Parmesan cheese over the eggplant and finally sprinkle on the parsley. Bake for 10 minutes.

PIZZA WITH ROASTED PEPPERS

MAKES ONE 12-INCH DOUBLE-CRUST PIZZA

Roasting peppers enhances their flavor, and once you've tried
them on pizza, they'll become a favorite. Because they are also
good in salads and on sandwiches, roast more than you need and
store the extras covered with olive oil in glass jars.

1 batch Garlic Dill Pizza Dough (see page 20)
1 red bell pepper
1 green pepper
1 yellow bell pepper
¾ cup Pizza Sauce (see page 28)
¾ cup fontina cheese, grated

◆ Preheat the oven to 500°.

◆ Cut the tops off the peppers and remove the seeds. Cut the peppers in half and then squash them so that they lay relatively flat (it's okay if the edges rip). Place the peppers, skin side up, in a broiler pan and broil for about eight minutes until blackened. Using tongs, place the peppers in a plastic bag. Seal and allow to cool. Once cooled, the skin will peel right off. Discard the skins. Slice the roasted peppers in long strips.

◆ Spread the pizza sauce on the pizza dough. Then decorate it with the pepper strips, alternating colors. There may be extra pepper strips, but cover them in olive oil, store in the refrigerator, and they'll keep for several days (use them on other pizzas or in salads). Lightly cover the peppers with the cheese. The cheese should not be so thick that the colorful peppers are obscured.

◆ Bake for 10 minutes.

PIZZA ROMANO

MAKES ONE 12-INCH DOUBLE-CRUST PIZZA

Polenta, an Italian version of corn meal, was used for a topping for
pizza in hard times when other ingredients weren't available. But
even in good times this one is worth eating. The cheese, corn meal,
and sauce make a tasty and hearty meal.

1 batch Basic Pizza Dough (see page 14)
½ cup corn meal
¼ tsp salt
1½ cups cold water
1 egg
½ cup Parmesan cheese, grated
⅔ cup Pizza Sauce (see page 28)

◆ Preheat oven to 500°.

◆ Put the corn meal and salt in a pan. Add
the cold water a little at a time, whisking it
in to remove all lumps. Place over moderate
heat and continue whisking until corn meal
thickens. When it gets too thick to whisk,
switch to a wooden spoon. Continue
stirring for about five minutes after the
corn meal thickens. Remove from the stove.
Beat the egg with ¼ cup of Parmesan
cheese. Stir into the corn meal mixture.

◆ To assemble the pizza, spread the pizza
sauce over the pizza dough. Spread the
corn meal mixture on top of the sauce,
using the back of a spoon to mash it down.
Top with the remaining Parmesan. Bake at
500° for 10 minutes.

PIZZA WITH TOMATO AND THREE CHEESES

MAKES ONE 12-INCH DOUBLE-CRUST PIZZA

The mellow creaminess of fontina and mozzarella combine with
the sharpness of Parmesan for a rich cheese pizza. Use a garlic dill
crust to add even more flavor.

1 batch Garlic Dill Pizza Dough (see page 20)
⅔ cup Pizza Sauce (see page 28)
½ cup grated mozzarella cheese
½ cup grated fontina cheese
¼ grated Parmesan cheese

◆ Preheat oven to 500°.

◆ Spread the pizza sauce onto the pizza
dough, leaving a ½-inch edge. Spread the
mozzarella, the fontina, and then the
Parmesan cheese over the sauce. Bake for
10 minutes.

Barbecued Pizza

❝❞❝❞❝❞

Makes one 12-inch double-crust pizza

Pizza can go on a picnic as easily as any other cook-out meal. Use a prebaked crust, or make your own stove-top, no-yeast crust, in a cast iron pan on top of a campfire. The smoky flavor you get when cooking outdoors enhances the flavor of the vegetables.

1 batch Whole Wheat Pizza Dough
  (see page 16)
wooden skewers
½ tsp brown sugar
½ tsp molasses
½ tsp vegetarian Worcestershire sauce
¾ cup Pizza Sauce (see page 28)
½ cup large mushrooms
½ medium red bell pepper
½ medium green pepper
¼ cup grated Romano cheese
¼ cup scallions, chopped
¾ cup mozzarella cheese, grated

◆ If you are making the pizza crust, preheat oven to 500° and bake the pizza dough for 25–30 minutes and remove from oven.

◆ Soak the wooden skewers in water to make them burn resistant.

◆ To make the sauce, stir the brown sugar, molasses, and Worcestershire sauce into the pizza sauce.

◆ Light the barbecue grill and allow the coals to get white hot. When the coals are ready, push them to the edge of the grill, leaving a clear 12-inch circle in the center.

◆ Cut the mushrooms in half and chop both bell peppers into pieces approximately one inch square. Run the skewers through them, leaving a little space between each to speed up cooking. Place the skewered vegetables in the center of the grill, cover, and barbecue five to seven minutes, turning once. Remove from the grill and set aside.

◆ Place the pizza crust in the center of the grill. Cover and barbecue for five minutes. Turn the crust over. Working fast, sprinkle the Romano over the crust. On top of that pour the pizza sauce. Then arrange the barbecued vegetables over the sauce. Top with the scallions and, finally, with the mozzarella. Cover and barbecue five to seven minutes or until cheese is melted.

❝❞❝❞❝❞

JAMBALAYA PIZZA

MAKES ONE 12-INCH DOUBLE-CRUST PIZZA

This spicy Cajun pizza makes use of the delicious meatless
sausages now on the market.

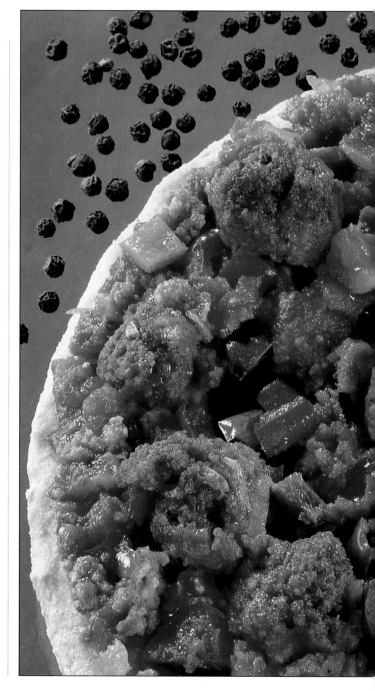

1 batch Corn Bread Pizza Dough
 (see page 17)
1 tbsp olive oil
2 cloves garlic, minced
2 medium onions, chopped
4 meatless sausage patties (4oz)
½ red bell pepper, chopped
½ green pepper, chopped
½ tsp oregano
¼ tsp white pepper
½ tsp salt
½ tsp cayenne pepper
½ tsp thyme
1 14.5-oz can tomatoes, drained, liquid
 reserved
¼ cup Cheddar cheese, grated

◆ Preheat oven to 500˚.
◆ Heat the oil in a pan and add the minced
garlic and chopped onion. Sauté a few
minutes until the onions begin to turn
opaque. Then crumble the sausages into
the pan. Add the red and green peppers
and the spices and sauté for five minutes
over high heat, stirring constantly. Drain
the tomatoes and reserve ½ cup of the
liquid. Chop the tomatoes and add them to
the pan along with the ½ cup of juice.
Simmer, stirring occasionally, until most of
the liquid is absorbed (about five minutes).
◆ To assemble the pizza, spread the
jambalaya over the pizza dough. Sprinkle
the cheese lightly over the top. Bake for 15
minutes. Serve immediately.

COLD
PIZZAS

ASIAN AVOCADO PIZZA

MAKES ONE 12-INCH DOUBLE-CRUST PIZZA

Horseradish and capers are the ingredients that give this avocado
salad an unusual kick. For an even more exotic salad, use black
sesame seeds instead of white. They can be found in Asian markets.

1 batch Chinese Pizza Dough
  (see page 20–21)
1 tbsp sesame seeds
2 large ripe avocados
2 Roma tomatoes, diced
2 tbsp horseradish
2 tsp crystallized ginger, minced
2 tbsp capers
3 tbsp cider vinegar
1 tbsp sugar

♦ Preheat the oven to 500°. Bake pizza
dough for 25–30 minutes, remove from
oven and allow to cool.

♦ Toast the sesame seeds in a non-stick pan
over medium high heat until browned,
about five minutes. Stir frequently to keep
from burning. Peel, seed, and dice the
avocados and place them in a bowl. Add
the diced tomatoes, horseradish, 1 teaspoon
of the toasted sesame seeds, ginger, and
capers. Stir gently to mix. In a separate
container, mix the vinegar and sugar. Pour
over the avocado mixture and gently toss.

♦ Spread the avocado salad on the cooled
crust. Top with the remaining toasted
sesame seeds. Serve chilled or at room
temperature.

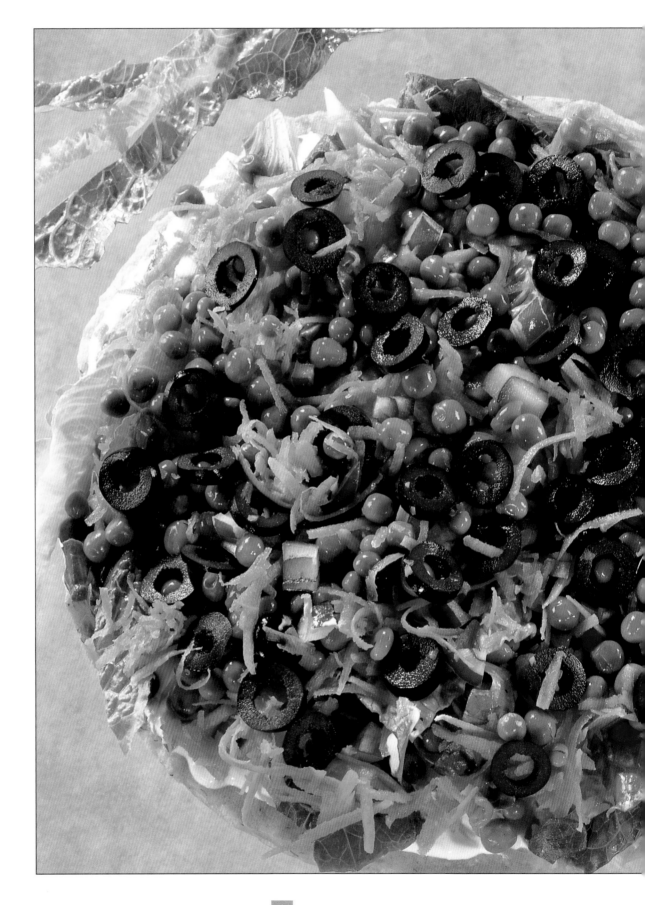

▶ Six-layer
Pizza.

SIX-LAYER PIZZA

MAKES ONE 12-INCH DOUBLE-CRUST PIZZA

Start with the sour cream and just layer the vegetables on top of one another. It's good for lunch or as a nutritious appetizer.

1 batch Garlic and Dill Pizza Dough
  (see page 20)
small lettuce, shredded
1 red onion, chopped
½ cup frozen peas, thawed to room
  temperature
1 carrot, grated
1 small jar (2.25 oz) sliced black olives
1 cup sour cream
salt and pepper to taste

◆ Preheat oven to 500°. Bake pizza dough for 25–30 minutes, remove from oven and allow to cool.
◆ Prepare the vegetables: shred the lettuce, chop the onions, thaw the peas, peel and grate the carrots. Drain the olives.
◆ To assemble the pizza, spread the sour cream on the prebaked, cooled crust. Then spread the shredded lettuce on top of the sour cream. Add the onions, then the carrots, then peas, and finally olives. Sprinkle salt and pepper. Serve cold.

AVOCADO AND ORANGE PIZZA

MAKES ONE 12-INCH DOUBLE-CRUST PIZZA

Oranges, avocados, and onions go well together with a sweet and sour dressing. Make sure the avocado is perfectly ripe. It should be soft, but not mushy.

1 batch Whole Wheat Cheese Pizza Dough
  (see page 17)
1 small sweet red onion, thinly sliced and
  separated into rings
1 large ripe avocado, peeled, and thinly sliced
1 11-oz can mandarin oranges, drained,
  1 tbsp of the liquid reserved
1 tsp salad oil
1 tsp balsamic vinegar
⅛ tsp dried mustard
½ tsp sugar
juice of ½ lemon
⅛ tsp salt

◆ Preheat oven to 500°. Bake pizza dough for 25–30 minutes, remove from oven and allow to cool.
◆ In a bowl, add red onion, avocado slices, and drained mandarin oranges. Gently toss. In a cup, mix the oil, vinegar, mustard, sugar, reserved orange juice, lemon juice, and salt. Whisk to blend well. Pour it over the avocado mixture and gently toss. Marinate the topping until ready to serve.
◆ To serve, spread the mixture over the cooled crust. Pour any remaining dressing on top.

PIZZA CRUDITÉ

MAKES ONE 12-INCH DOUBLE-CRUST PIZZA

Fresh dill enhances the taste of the creamy sauce. Chop the
vegetables very finely for best results. This pizza makes a good
leftover as the flavors seem to blend when left overnight
in the refrigerator.

1 batch Garlic Dill Pizza Dough (see page 20)
6 oz cream cheese, softened
½ cup mayonnaise
1 tsp fresh dill, snipped into small pieces
1 clove garlic, minced (½ tsp)
¼ tsp salt
4 medium carrots
1 medium ripe tomato
1 red onion
1 2.25-oz jar sliced black olives, drained

◈ Preheat the oven to 500°. Bake the pizza
dough for 25–30 minutes, remove from
oven and allow to cool.

◈ In a bowl, cream the softened cream
cheese and mayonnaise together, mashing
well with a fork. Add the fresh dill, minced
garlic, and salt and mix thoroughly. Using a
rubber spatula, spread this mixture onto the
cooled, cooked crust.

◈ Peel the carrots and chop them very
finely. Also finely chop the tomato and
onion. Mix the chopped vegetables in a
bowl along with the drained olives. Pile the
vegetables onto the pizza and refrigerate for
at least a half hour before serving.

SWEET AND SOUR CORN PIZZA

This colorful pizza makes an unusual appetizer. It is sweet and best served in small slices. Make the topping ahead of time and store it in the refrigerator so that the flavors have time to blend.

1 batch Jalapeño-Tomato Pizza Dough
   (see page 18)

½ tsp turmeric

½ tsp salt

½ tsp dry mustard

¼ cup cider vinegar

¼ cup sugar

1 10-oz can niblet corn

1 sweet onion, chopped

½ green pepper, chopped

½ red bell pepper, chopped

1 jalapeño pepper, seeded and finely
   chopped

1 tbsp cornstarch

8 oz feta cheese, crumbled

◆ Preheat the oven to 500°. Bake the pizza dough for 25–30 minutes, remove from oven and allow to cool.

◆ Put the turmeric, salt, mustard, vinegar, and sugar in a pan and stir over medium heat until the sugar and spices are dissolved. Add the corn, onions, red, green, and jalapeño peppers and bring to a boil. Reduce heat and simmer for 15 minutes, stirring occasionally.

◆ Drain a little of the hot liquid from the mixture into a cup and add the cornstarch, stirring to a smooth paste. Stir this mixture back into the pan and cook until corn relish thickens. Allow to cool and store in the refrigerator overnight to allow flavors to blend. (This is important. The relish is too tart when freshly made.)

◆ To make the pizza, spread the relish over the cool crust, leaving an inch around the edge. Top with the crumbled feta and serve.

Corn and Tomato Pizza

Makes one 12-inch double-crust pizza

Southwestern cuisine comes to mind when you make this colorful corn and tomato pizza. The jalapeño pepper adds a little kick. Chopped cilantro is a southwestern substitute for parsley.

1 batch Basic or Whole Wheat Pizza Dough
   (see page 14 or 16)
1 l-lb can corn, drained
1 red onion, diced
1 jalapeño pepper, minced (about 1 tbsp)
½ red bell pepper, diced
1 medium-sized fresh tomato, diced
½ cup chopped cilantro
1 tsp salt
juice of ½ lemon
3 tbsp olive oil
1 tsp tarragon
1 tsp Dijon-style mustard
¼ tsp pepper

◆ Preheat the oven to 500˚. Bake the pizza dough for 25–30 minutes, remove from oven and allow to cool.

◆ Drain the corn and place it in a bowl. Add the diced onions, minced jalapeño pepper, diced red bell pepper, diced tomato, chopped cilantro, and salt. Stir gently to mix.

◆ In a separate bowl, squeeze the lemon juice and add the olive oil. Whisk until well combined. Add the tarragon, mustard, and pepper and whisk again to blend. Pour the dressing over the corn mixture, stirring gently to coat.

◆ Using a slotted spoon, spread the corn and tomato salad over the pizza. Pour about 1 tablespoon of the dressing over the top. If making ahead of time, refrigerate the salad and spread it over the crust right before serving. Can be served chilled or at room temperature.

FRUIT SALAD PIZZA

MAKES ONE 12-INCH DOUBLE-CRUST PIZZA

Creamy pineapple yogurt is used as a dressing to make this recipe special. Serve it during the summer when melons are at their peak of ripeness. Try other types of fruit such as papayas or mangos.

1 batch Basic Pizza Dough (see page 14)
½ honeydew melon
1½ cantaloupe
1 cup fresh pineapple
6 strawberries
3½ oz Gouda cheese (half a round), diced
½ tsp ground ginger
juice of 1 lime
8 oz pineapple yogurt
½ cup blueberries

◆ Preheat oven to 500°. Bake pizza dough for about 25–30 minutes, remove from oven and allow to cool.

◆ Cut both melons in half and remove the seeds. Dice into small squares and place in a bowl. Peel the pineapple and remove the core. Dice in small squares and add to the bowl. Add the strawberries, stems removed, and berries cut in half (smaller if they are large). Cut the Gouda round in half. Remove the wax and dice the cheese. Add to the bowl. Sprinkle the ginger and squeeze the lime juice over the fruit and cheese. Gently fold in the yogurt. Store in the refrigerator until ready to serve.

◆ To assemble the pizza, spread the fruit mixture gently over the prebaked, cooled crust. Top with the blueberries.

➤ Three-bean Pizza.

THREE-BEAN PIZZA

MAKES ONE 12-INCH DOUBLE-CRUST PIZZA

Use any three types of beans for variation. Canned beans are easy and quick, but you could use dried beans. Soak and cook them ahead of time and allow them to cool.

1 batch Jalapeño-Tomato Pizza Dough
  (see page 18)
⅔ cup canned pinto beans
⅔ cup canned garbanzo beans
⅔ cup canned black beans
1 red onion, sliced
½ cup green pepper, diced

1 medium tomato, chopped
1 tsp cider vinegar
½ tsp salt
¼ tsp pepper
1 tsp Dijon-style mustard
1 tbsp mayonnaise

◆ Preheat the oven to 500°. Bake the pizza dough for 25–30 minutes, remove from oven and allow to cool.

◆ Drain and rinse the beans and place them in a bowl. Slice the onions into circles, separate into rings, then cut in half. Add them to the bowl. Add the diced green pepper and chopped tomato. In a separate container, mix the vinegar, salt, pepper, mustard, and mayonnaise. Then add this mixture to the vegetables, stirring gently to coat. Avoid mashing the beans.

◆ Spread the mixture on the crust and refrigerate for half an hour before serving.

PIZZAS WITH TOFU

TOFU AND VEGETABLE PIZZA

MAKES ONE 12-INCH DOUBLE-CRUST PIZZA

Tofu with vegetables, a popular vegetarian combination in
Vietnamese cooking, make a satisfying meal on a pizza crust.

1 batch Garlic Dill Pizza Dough (see page 20)

¼ cup soy sauce

3½ tbsp rice wine vinegar

2 cloves garlic, minced

¼ tsp cumin

1 tsp fresh grated ginger

2 tsp peanut oil

6 oz tofu

2 broccoli flowerets

2 carrots, peeled and sliced

½ cup water chestnuts, sliced

◆ Preheat the oven to 500°. Bake the pizza dough for five minutes.

◆ Mix the soy sauce, vinegar, minced garlic, cumin, fresh ginger, and peanut oil together. Dice the tofu into ½-inch squares and place in a bowl. Pour the soy sauce mixture over the tofu, stirring to coat.

◆ Add the broccoli flowerets, sliced carrots, and sliced chestnuts to the tofu mixture, stirring to coat. Spread the mixture over the crust and bake for five minutes.

CURRIED TOFU PIZZA

MAKES ONE 12-INCH DOUBLE-CRUST PIZZA

Curry sauce is always spicy, but can be either hot or mild. This
version uses mild curry powder, but you can substitute to
your own taste.

1 batch Rye Bread Pizza Dough
   (see page 22–23)

¼ cup butter

2 onions, chopped

4 tsp turmeric

4 tsp curry powder

½ tsp cloves

1 tsp white pepper

2 tsp salt

2 tsp dried mint

2 tbsp crystallized ginger, finely chopped

juice of 2 limes

¼ cup coconut milk (preferably unsweetened)

12 oz tofu, diced

4 tbsp raisins

◆ Preheat the oven to 500°. Bake the rye bread pizza dough for five minutes.

◆ Melt the butter in a pan and sauté the onions until soft, about five minutes. Remove from the heat and add the spices, mint, finely chopped ginger, lime juice, and coconut milk. Return to the heat and simmer for about five minutes, stirring until mixture is blended and slightly thick. Remove from the heat and add the tofu and raisins, stirring gently to coat the tofu completely.

◆ Spread the curried tofu mixture on the prebaked crust, leaving a ½-inch edge. Bake for five minutes.

▲ Tofu and Vegetable Pizza.

CHILI PIZZA

MAKES ONE 12-INCH DOUBLE-CRUST PIZZA

Chili pizza is perfect to serve at a Super Bowl party because it combines two favorite football foods, pizza and chili. You can increase the heat by adding more jalapeños, or by using "Hot Mexican" chili powder.

1 batch Corn Bread Pizza Dough
  (see page 17)
1 tbsp olive oil
1 onion, chopped
¾ cup chopped green peppers
2 large cloves garlic, minced
1 jalapeño pepper, minced
1 1-lb can peeled tomatoes, drained, ¼ cup
  liquid reserved
1 tbsp chili powder
½ tsp cumin
½ tsp oregano
½ tsp salt
½ tsp curry powder
6 oz tofu
1 cup canned dark red kidney beans, drained
⅔ cup Cheddar cheese, grated

◆ Preheat the oven to 500°.

◆ Heat the oil in a pan and sauté the chopped onions, green peppers, garlic, and jalapeños until onions are soft. Drain the tomatoes, reserving the liquid, and chop them into small pieces. Add them to the pan along with ¼ cup of the reserved liquid. Add the spices. Dice the tofu into pieces about 1 inch square. Add to the pan and simmer for about five minutes, until most of the liquid is evaporated. Remove from the heat and add the kidney beans.

◆ Spread the chili on the corn bread pizza dough. Top with Cheddar cheese. Bake for 15 minutes at 500°.

SWEET AND SOUR TOFU PIZZA

MAKES ONE 12-INCH DOUBLE-CRUST PIZZA

Sweet and sour dishes are popular Chinese fare that go just as easily on pizza crust as they do on rice. This adaptation of the stir-fry favorite is a colorful medley of fruit, vegetables, and tofu in a tangy sauce.

1 batch Chinese Pizza Dough
  (see page 20–21)
2 tsp soy sauce
2 tsp sugar
2 tsp white wine vinegar
1 tsp cornstarch
¼ tsp ground ginger
2 tsp catsup
2 tsp peanut oil
8 oz tofu
1 onion, chopped
1 tomato, chopped
1 cup green pepper, chopped
½ cup canned pineapple, drained, chopped

◆ Preheat the oven to 500°.
◆ Combine the soy sauce, sugar, vinegar, cornstarch, ginger, catsup, and oil in a bowl and stir to mix well. Dice the tofu into small cubes and add to the sauce, stirring gently to coat. Coarsely chop the onions, tomato, and green pepper and add them to the tofu. Chop the pineapple into bite-sized pieces and stir into the tofu mixture. Pile onto the pizza dough and bake for 10 minutes.

SESAME TOFU PIZZA

MAKES ONE 12-INCH DOUBLE-CRUST PIZZA

The sesame-coated tofu squares that top this pizza are crunchy on
the outside, tangy and soft on the inside. The canned baby corn,
cut into thin rounds, looks like edible flowers.

1 batch Chinese Pizza Dough
  (see page 20–21)
6 oz tofu
⅓ cup teriyaki sauce
¼ cup whole wheat flour
¼ cup sesame seeds
¼ cup oil
4 oz canned baby corn
4 scallions

◆ Preheat the oven to 500°.
◆ Drain the tofu and cut into domino-sized
pieces (1 x 1½ x ¼ inches). Marinate in the
teriyaki sauce for 15 minutes, turning to
coat. In a separate bowl, mix the flour and
sesame seeds.
◆ When the tofu has marinated, remove
with a slotted spoon, saving the marinade
for later use. Coat the tofu pieces with the
sesame seed mixture. Heat the oil in a pan
and then fry the coated tofu until lightly
brown, two or three minutes per side.
◆ Using a slotted spoon, remove the tofu
from the pan and place on top of the
unbaked pizza crust. Sprinkle with the corn
stars and then the chopped scallions. Spoon
3 tablespoons of the marinade over the
dough. Bake at 500° for 10 minutes.

TOFU AND CASHEW PIZZA

MAKES ONE 12-INCH DOUBLE-CRUST PIZZA

Be sure to use fresh grated ginger in this recipe because it adds a
distinctive flavor. Cashews are added in the last five minutes of
baking to prevent them from burning.

1 batch Chinese Pizza Dough
  (see page 20–21)
juice of 1 lemon
4 tsp tomato paste
4 tsp honey
3 tbsp soy sauce

3 cloves garlic, minced
1 tbsp grated fresh ginger
10 oz tofu
6 scallions, whites and greens
4 carrots, peeled
4 oz salted cashews

◆ Preheat the oven to 500˚.

◆ In a bowl, squeeze the lemon juice and add the tomato paste, honey, soy sauce, minced garlic, and grated fresh ginger. Slice the tofu into small cubes and add to the sauce, stirring gently to coat. Chop the scallions and slice the carrots into rounds and add them to the tofu mixture. Spread onto the pizza dough. Bake for five minutes. Then top with the cashews and bake for five more minutes taking care not to burn them.

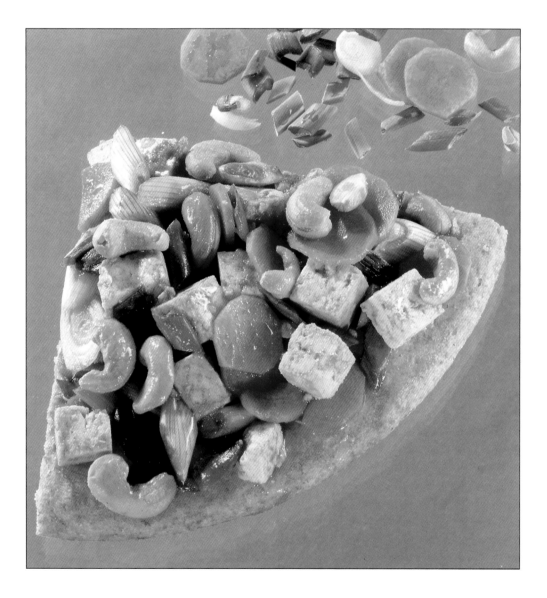

▲ Tofu and Cashew Pizza.

TOFU IN PEANUT SAUCE PIZZA

MAKES ONE 12-INCH DOUBLE-CRUST PIZZA

Peanut butter and coconut milk combine to make a delicious
peanut sauce from Thailand in this pizza variation. Chow mein
noodles, added right before serving, add crunch to the cooked
vegetables and tofu.

1 batch Chinese Pizza Dough
  (see page 20–21)
⅓ cup unsweetened coconut milk
¼ cup smooth peanut butter
2 tsp sugar
1 tsp grated fresh ginger
2 cloves garlic, minced
2 cups spinach, shredded
2 tsp peanut oil
½ cup alfalfa sprouts
4 scallions, chopped
4 oz firm-style tofu
⅔ cup chow mein noodles, to garnish

◆ Preheat the oven to 500°.

◆ In a small pan, heat the coconut milk,
peanut butter, sugar (omit sugar if using
sweetened coconut milk), grated ginger,
and garlic until blended. Allow to simmer,
stirring frequently, while assembling the
vegetables.

◆ Wash and tear the spinach into small
pieces. Pour the oil over the spinach and
toss. Add the alfalfa sprouts and chopped
scallions. Add the tofu, sliced into ½-inch
squares. Toss gently to mix.

◆ Spread the tofu and vegetables over the
pizza dough. Top with the sauce. Spread it
over the tofu mixture with the back of a
spoon. Bake for 10 minutes.

◆ Remove from the oven when done.
Plunge the chow mein noodles into boiling
water, about 3 minutes, and drain. Arrange
on top of the pizza. Serve immediately.

PIZZAS
WITH UNUSUAL
VEGETABLES

▚▚▚▚▚

SWISS GREEN BEAN PIZZA

MAKES ONE 12-INCH DOUBLE-CRUST PIZZA

Try this pizza when green beans are in season, especially if they come from your own garden. It turns an ordinary vegetable into a treat.

1 batch Whole Wheat Pizza Dough
  (see page 16)
1 lb fresh green beans
2 tbsp olive oil
½ cup sliced almonds
1 cup grated Swiss cheese

⬥ Preheat the oven to 500°.
⬥ Wash and snip off the ends of the green beans. Steam them for five to seven minutes, until crisp-tender. Then arrange the beans on the pizza dough. Sprinkle the olive oil over the beans. Next, sprinkle on the sliced almonds and top with the Swiss cheese. Bake for 10 minutes.

SESAME VEGETABLE PIZZA

MAKES ONE 12-INCH DOUBLE-CRUST PIZZA

Vegetables sprinkled with sesame seeds is a dish one might find in Malaysia. This easy-to-assemble pizza is very healthful, using minimal oil and lots of fresh vegetables.

1 batch Garlic Dill Pizza Dough (see page 20)
½ medium cucumber, seeded
2 carrots, chopped
¼ head cauliflower
1 tbsp olive oil
1 tbsp soy sauce
2 tsp sesame seeds

⬥ Preheat oven to 500°.
⬥ Cut the peeled cucumber in half lengthwise and scoop out the seeds. Thinly slice along the width into semicircles. Peel and slice the carrots into thin circles. Separate the cauliflower into small flowerets.
⬥ To assemble the pizza, start with the cucumbers. Add the carrots on top of them and then the cauliflower. Sprinkle the olive oil and then the soy sauce over the vegetables. Finish with the sesame seeds.
⬥ Bake for about 10 minutes.

▶ Swiss Green
Bean Pizza.

SPINACH AND CHEESE PIZZA

MAKES ONE 12-INCH DOUBLE-CRUST PIZZA

Dried mint and feta cheese dress up ordinary spinach in this pizza
and bring to mind a Greek salad. But this dish is served
hot and steaming.

1 batch Garlic Dill Pizza Dough (see page 20)

2 tbsp olive oil

1 onion, chopped

2 large garlic cloves, minced

1 10-oz package frozen, chopped spinach,
   thawed

¼ tsp salt

½ tsp basil

½ tsp oregano

½ tsp dried mint

juice of 1 lemon

¾ cup grated mozzarella

2 medium tomatoes, sliced

¾ cup feta cheese, crumbled

◆ Preheat oven to 500°.

◆ Heat the olive oil in a pan, add the
chopped onions and minced garlic, and
sauté until the onions are opaque (about
five minutes). Drain the spinach, then add
to the pan along with the spices and the
lemon juice. Simmer until all of the liquid
has evaporated.

◆ Using a slotted spoon to remove it from
the pan, spread the spinach mixture over
the pizza dough, leaving ½ inch around the
edge. Layer the mozzarella over the
spinach, followed by the tomatoes sliced
into fairly thin rounds. Top the tomatoes
with the feta.

◆ Bake the pizza for 10 minutes.

BLUE CHEESE AND BROCCOLI PIZZA

MAKES ONE 12-INCH DOUBLE-CRUST PIZZA

When creamy blue cheese melts on the top of this pizza, it turns ordinary broccoli into a treat. The pecans add to the delight.

1 batch Garlic Dill Pizza Dough (see page 20)

1 small head of broccoli, separated into flowerets

small white onion, thinly sliced

1 tbsp olive oil

⅓ cup pecans, chopped

4 oz blue cheese, crumbled

◆ Preheat oven to 500°.

◆ Remove the stem from the broccoli; separate the head into small flowerets. You need about 2 cups. To assemble the pizza, first lay the thinly sliced onion over the pizza dough. Then add the broccoli. Sprinkle the olive oil over the vegetables. Add the pecans and top with the crumbled blue cheese.

◆ Bake in the lower half of the oven for about 6 minutes.

SPLIT PEA PIZZA

▪▪▪▪▪▪

MAKES ONE 12-INCH DOUBLE-CRUST PIZZA

This pizza makes a hearty dinner on a cold winter night. A tossed salad and a cold beer completes the meal.

1 batch Corn Bread Pizza Dough
   (see page 17)
½ cup dried split peas
2¼ cups water, divided
¼ cup vegetable oil
¼ cup whole wheat flour
½ tsp salt
¼ tsp nutmeg
¼ tsp dry mustard
½ tsp vegetarian Worcestershire sauce
1 tbsp tomato paste
1 cup sharp Cheddar cheese, grated
1 2-oz jar chopped pimientos, drained

◆ Preheat oven to 500˚. Bake the pizza dough for five minutes and remove from the oven.

◆ Rinse the dried peas in cold water. Put them in a pan with 1 cup of water and bring to a boil. Reduce to low and simmer for about 20 minutes until peas are soft but not mushy. Liquid should be absorbed, but drain the peas if necessary.

◆ In a separate pan, heat the oil and add the flour, stirring to make a roux. Slowly add the remaining 1¼ cups water and stir, mixing well. Add the salt, nutmeg, mustard, Worcestershire sauce, and tomato paste. Simmer for five minutes, stirring frequently. Sauce should be fairly thick. Add the cheese, stirring until it melts. Stir in the drained peas and remove from heat.

◆ Top the prebaked crust with the peas, leaving ½ inch around the edge. Dot the split peas with the drained pimientos. Bake for 10 minutes.

◀ Blue Cheese
and Broccoli
Pizza.

▪▪▪▪▪▪

CHEESE AND ARTICHOKE PIZZA

MAKES ONE 12-INCH DOUBLE-CRUST PIZZA

Artichoke hearts bottled in olive oil are already marinated. There
is little the cook has to do but assemble the ingredients and bake
them to produce a perfectly seasoned pizza.

1 batch Whole Wheat Pizza Dough
  (see page 16)
1 10-oz bottle artichoke hearts
⅔ cup shredded mozzarella cheese
⅔ cup grated fresh Romano cheese
2 cloves garlic, minced
1 2-oz jar sliced pimientos, drained

◈ Preheat oven to 500˚.
◈ Drain the artichoke hearts, reserving the
liquid. Finely chop the artichoke and place
in a bowl. Add both cheeses, garlic, and
drained pimientos. Measure ¼ cup of the
reserved liquid from the artichoke hearts
and add it to the bowl. Stir to mix.
◈ Top the pizza dough with the artichoke/
cheese mixture and bake for 10 minutes,
until cheese is melted.

PIZZA CAPONATA

MAKES ONE 12-INCH DOUBLE-CRUST PIZZA

Caponata, an eggplant-based mixture, is good served either hot or
cold. The flavor seems to improve when it is marinated overnight.
So you can make it ahead of time and serve it hot, or on a
precooked crust as a pizza salad.

1 batch Basic Pizza Dough (see page 14)
1 medium eggplant, peeled and chopped
6 tbsp olive oil, divided
1 large garlic clove, pressed
1 onion, chopped
2 tbsp water
2 celery stalks, diced

¼ cup Pizza Sauce (see page 18) (or substitute
  canned tomato sauce)
2 tbsp capers
2 oz pimiento-stuffed olives, drained and
  halved
2 tsp sugar
1 tbsp red wine vinegar

◆ Preheat oven to 500°.

◆ Peel and dice the eggplant and sauté it in four tablespoons of the oil for about five minutes until slightly browned. Remove from the pan. Heat the remaining oil and sauté the garlic and onions until onions are limp. Add the diced celery, pizza sauce, and water. Simmer until celery is soft (about 10 minutes). Add the eggplant back into the pan. Stir in the capers, olives, sugar, and vinegar. Simmer for an additional five minutes.

◆ Spread the caponata onto the pizza dough. Bake for 10 minutes at 500°.

◀ Pizza Caponata.

PIZZA MONTE CARLO

This pizza is named after Monte Carlo because of its class, not its richness. Asparagus is one of the tastiest vegetables to eat fresh. If it is not in season, however, you can substitute a 9-ounce package of frozen asparagus pieces. Thaw to room temperature before rolling in the cheese.

1 batch Whole Wheat Pizza Dough
    (see page 16)
1 tbsp olive oil
2½ cups chopped mushrooms
1 2-oz jar diced pimientos, drained
1 lb fresh asparagus
⅓ cup grated Romano cheese
juice of ½ lemon

◆ Preheat oven to 500˚.

◆ Heat the oil in a pan and sauté the mushrooms for about five minutes until limp. Remove from the heat and stir in the drained pimientos.

◆ Snap off the tough ends of the asparagus and steam until crisp-tender. Chop into two-inch pieces and roll them in the Romano cheese.

◆ To assemble the pizza, spread the mushroom mixture over the pizza dough. Top with the asparagus and cheese. Squeeze the lemon juice over the pizza. Bake for 10 minutes.

BEETS IN ORANGE SAUCE PIZZA

MAKES ONE 12-INCH DOUBLE-CRUST PIZZA

Beets, while not a popular vegetable, are an excellent source of beta carotene. Topped with a sweet orange sauce and piled on a corn bread crust, they become a dish one can really enjoy.

1 batch Corn Bread Pizza Dough
  (see page 17)
1 lb fresh beets, greens removed
2 tbsp cornstarch
1 cup orange juice
6 tbsp sugar
⅛ tsp salt
sprig of mint for garnish

◆ Preheat the oven to 500°.
◆ Boil the beets for about 40 minutes until they can be easily pierced with a fork. Allow them to cool and then peel. Thinly slice and arrange on the pizza dough.
◆ In a separate pan, mix the cornstarch, orange juice, sugar, and salt. Bring to a boil, stirring constantly until mixture thickens, about five minutes. Pour the sauce over the beets. Bake for 15 minutes. Garnish with a sprig of mint before serving.

HERBED BRUSSELS SPROUTS AND CARROT PIZZA

MAKES ONE 12-INCH DOUBLE-CRUST PIZZA

This colorful pizza makes interesting use of an unusual vegetable. Serve it as an appetizer, a side dish, or as part of a buffet.

1 batch Rye Bread Pizza Dough
  (see page 22–23)
7–8 oz Brussels sprouts
4 oz baby carrots, peeled
juice of 1 lemon
2 tbsp olive oil
1 tsp dried tarragon
¼ tsp ground nutmeg

◆ Preheat the oven to 500°. Bake the pizza dough for three minutes.
◆ Rinse the brussels sprouts, remove the stems and cut in half lengthwise. Slice any baby carrots that are larger than about ¼-inch in diameter in half lengthwise. Steam vegetables for four minutes.
◆ In a separate bowl, whisk together the lemon juice, olive oil, and spices.
◆ Arrange the brussels sprouts and carrots alternately on the prebaked crust in a colorful pattern. Pour the lemon juice mixture over the vegetables. Bake for seven to eight minutes.

▲ Herbed Brussels Sprouts and
Carrot Pizza.

DEEP DISH RATATOUILLE PIZZA

MAKES ONE 9 x 13-INCH DEEP-DISH PIZZA

Ratatouille is an eggplant and zucchini casserole that works well
piled into a deep dish pizza. Most of its ingredients, including the
fresh basil, can be grown in a backyard garden.

1 batch Basic or Whole Wheat Pizza Dough
  (see page 14 or 16)
1 small eggplant, chopped
1 tbsp + ½ tsp salt
1 small green pepper
1 small onion, chopped
1 medium zucchini
1 large tomato
2 cloves garlic, minced
¼ cup fresh basil leaves
¼ tsp pepper
¼ cup olive oil

◆ Preheat oven to 500°.

◆ Peel the eggplant. Slice into ½-inch thick
rounds. Soak in a bowl of water and 1
tablespoon salt for 20 minutes. Then rinse
well and press between paper towels to dry.
Dice the eggplant into pieces approximately
½ inch square. Dice the green pepper and
onion. Slice the zucchini into rounds, and
then cut each round into fourths. Coarsely
chop the tomato.

◆ Put the chopped and diced vegetables in
a bowl and stir in the minced garlic. Add
the fresh basil chopped or torn into small
pieces. Then add ½ teaspoon salt, pepper,
and olive oil. Stir gently to mix.

◆ Place the dough in the center of a lightly
oiled 13 x 9 x 2-inch pan. Using your
fingers, gently spread the dough until it
covers the bottom of the pan evenly and
goes halfway up the sides.

◆ Empty the contents of the bowl onto the
dough and spread evenly over the bottom.
Bake for 20 minutes.

PIZZA VERDE

MAKES ONE 12-INCH DOUBLE-CRUST PIZZA

The tomatillo is a familiar ingredient in southwestern cuisine and is the basis for green sauces. Its name means "little tomato" in Spanish, and it looks like a small green tomato in a brown, papery husk. Although tomatillos aren't actually tomatoes, they have a similar taste to green tomatoes, which can be substituted in this recipe.

1 batch Whole Wheat Cheese Pizza Dough
   (see page 17)
1½ lb fresh tomatillos
¼ cup vegetable oil
2 large clove garlic, minced
2 tsp cumin
1 small dried red pepper, crushed
1 onion, chopped
¼ tsp sugar
⅛ tsp ground cloves
3 Roma tomatoes, thinly sliced
¾ cup grated white Cheddar cheese

◆ Preheat oven to 500˚.

◆ Soak the tomatillos in warm water for about 10 minutes until husks are softened. Remove husks and rinse the tomatillos clean under cool water. Cut them in slices about ⅛–¼ inch thick.

◆ In a pan, heat the oil over medium heat. Add the garlic, cumin, and red pepper and stir until well mixed and aromatic (about three minutes). Add the onions and sauté until limp (about five minutes). Add the tomatillos, sugar, and cloves and cook over low heat for about 20 minutes. Tomatillos should be limp, but still retain their shape.

◆ To assemble the pizza, spread the sauce over the pizza dough. Place the tomatoes on top of the sauce. Top with the white Cheddar cheese. Bake for 10 minutes.

FENNEL MORNAY PIZZA

Fennel has been used for years in Italian cooking, but only recently has it become available in supermarkets in the U.S. This anise-flavored bulb blends smoothly with a mornay sauce made from Gruyère cheese.

1 batch Rye Bread Pizza Dough (see page 22)
1 fennel bulb
6 carrots
3 tbsp butter
3 tbsp flour
¾ cup liquid from vegetables
⅓ cup half and half
3 oz Gruyère, cut up
⅓ cup Parmesan
¼ tsp salt
¼ tsp white pepper
2 tsp dried thyme

◆ Preheat oven to 500°.

◆ Cut and discard the fennel tops off the bulb and coarsely chop (you can include the stalks). Peel the carrots. Put the fennel and carrots in a pot and cover them with water. Boil the vegetables until tender (10 to 15 minutes). Check the doneness by inserting a fork into them. They should be soft, but not mushy. Drain the vegetables, reserving ¾ cup of the liquid. Allow them to cool and then chop into small pieces.

◆ To make the sauce, melt the butter in a saucepan over low heat. Add the flour and stir until smooth. Add the reserved liquid from the vegetables and turn up the heat to high. Bring to a boil and add the half and half, stirring frequently to blend. Cook for several minutes until thickened. Add the Gruyère pieces and Parmesan to the sauce and stir while the cheeses melt. Stir in the salt and pepper.

◆ To assemble the pizza, spread the fennel and carrot mixture over the pizza dough. Pour the sauce over the vegetables and sprinkle with the dried thyme. Bake at 500° for 10 minutes.

CHAYOTE PIZZA

Chayote is a member of the squash family and is also known as merlot. It has a very mild flavor and a texture somewhat like a pear. It takes on the flavor of whatever sauce or spices it is cooked with.

1 batch Jalapeño-Tomato Pizza Dough
  (see page 18)
2 chayote or other small squash, diced
1 tbsp coriander
1 tbsp cumin
½ tsp salt
12 baby carrots, peeled and sliced
1 onion, chopped
2 jalapeño peppers, minced
2 tbsp olive oil
¾ cup Swiss cheese, grated

◆ Preheat the oven to 500°.
◆ Cut the end off each squash and discard. Cut the squash in half and remove the seeds in the center. Chop into ½-inch squares and place in a bowl. Add the coriander, cumin, and salt and stir the squash until well coated by the spices. Add the chopped peeled carrots, chopped onions, and minced jalapeño peppers and stir. Finally, stir in the oil.
◆ Spread the chayote mixture on the pizza dough, leaving a ½-inch edge. Spread the grated cheese over the top. Bake for 10 minutes.

THAI VEGETABLE PIZZA

Coconut milk added to the sauce makes this vegetable pizza reminiscent of Thai cooking. Fresh basil is much more flavorful and aromatic than dried, so use it whenever possible.

1 batch Chinese Pizza Dough
  (see page 20–21)
1 oz dried mushrooms
1 small zucchini
1 small white onion
½ red bell pepper
large handful fresh basil leaves

2 tbsp canned unsweetened coconut milk
4 tsp sugar
½ tsp ground ginger
2 tsp soy sauce
1 tbsp peanut oil

➤ Thai
Vegetable
Pizza.

◆ Preheat oven to 500°.

◆ Soak the mushrooms in warm water until softened (about 15 minutes). Drain and squeeze them to remove as much moisture as possible. Cut into bite-sized pieces. Chop the zucchini into thin rounds and cut the rounds in half. Coarsely chop the onion and dice the red pepper. Wash and chop (or cut with scissors) basil leaves. Mix mushrooms, vegetables, and basil in a bowl.

◆ In a separate bowl, combine coconut milk and sugar (omit the sugar if using sweetened coconut milk), ginger, and soy sauce and mix thoroughly. Stir into the vegetable mixture.

◆ Spread the mixture onto the pizza dough and sprinkle with the peanut oil. Bake for 10 minutes.

SPECIALTY PIZZAS

▀▀▀▀▀

PIZZA PRIMAVERA

"Sinfully rich" is how this pizza can be described with its sauce made of heavy cream and cheese. But it's also loaded with healthy fresh vegetables.

1 batch Whole Wheat Pizza Dough (see page 16)

3 tsp olive oil

3 tsp flour

1 cup heavy cream

½ cup loosely packed basil leaves, finely chopped

2 cloves garlic, minced

2 scallions, chopped

½ cup Parmesan cheese

8 oz fresh asparagus, chopped

½ large red bell pepper

1 small onion, chopped

1 small zucchini

◆ Preheat oven to 500°.

◆ Bake the pizza dough for three minutes and remove from oven.

◆ To make the sauce, heat the olive oil in a pan and add the flour, stirring to blend. Allow to cook for two or three minutes until bubbling. Slowly add the cream, stirring to mix. When the flour mixture is smooth, add the basil, garlic, and scallions. Bring to a boil and then simmer over low heat for five minutes, stirring frequently. Remove from the heat and stir in the Parmesan cheese.

◆ Wash the asparagus and snap off the ends, and then chop on the diagonal into 2-inch pieces. Seed and chop the bell pepper into 2-inch squares. Chop the onions and zucchini into fairly small pieces. Toss the vegetables in a bowl to mix.

◆ To assemble the pizza, spread the vegetables on the prebaked crust. Pour the sauce over the vegetables, spreading it with a back of a spoon if necessary. Bake for seven to eight minutes.

GREEK PIZZA

If you grow mint in your garden, you know it has a tendency to take over. But when you have recipes like this to make, you don't mind having lots of it on hand.

1 batch Basic or Whole Wheat Pizza Dough
   (see page 14 or 16)
1½ cups loosely packed fresh mint
1 tbsp olive oil
1 6 oz can pitted sliced black olives
2 oz feta cheese, crumbled

◆ Preheat oven to 500°.
◆ Roughly chop the mint leaves and place in a bowl with the olive oil; stir to coat. Set aside for a few minutes. Drain the olives and spread them over the pizza dough. Then spread the mint mixture, pouring any extra oil on the pizza. Top with the feta.
◆ Bake for eight minutes.

PIZZA RAREBIT

Beer gives a special flavor to this adaptation of the old Welsh dish. The original version can be served on grilled tomatoes, but in this recipe, tomatoes are the topper.

1 batch Rye Bread Pizza Dough
   (see page 22–23)
¼ cup butter
¼ cup flour
½ tsp vegetarian Worcestershire sauce
½ tsp salt
½ tsp pepper
½ tsp dry mustard
⅓ cup milk
⅓ cup beer
1¼ cups grated Cheddar cheese
½ large tomato, sliced
½ tsp paprika

◆ Preheat oven to 500°. Bake pizza dough for five minutes and remove from oven.
◆ Melt the butter in a saucepan over medium heat. Add the flour, Worcestershire sauce, salt, pepper, and dry mustard and stir until blended. Add the milk and cook, stirring constantly, until mixture is smooth and thick. Add the beer and stir until mixture is again smooth. Simmer for three or four minutes. Add the Cheddar cheese until melted and blended in.
◆ Spread the mixture over the pre-baked crust, leaving a ½-inch edge. Slice the tomato into thin rounds and arrange about eight slices on top of the pizza. Sprinkle with paprika and bake for five minutes.

◄ Greek Pizza.

APPLE AND BRIE PIZZA

MAKES ONE 12-INCH DOUBLE-CRUST PIZZA

Apples and cheese have always gone well together. This recipe
adds the crunch of almonds to the creaminess of the melted Brie.

1 batch Basic Pizza Dough (see page 14)
1 tart green apple such as Granny Smith
8 oz Brie
¼ cup sliced almonds

◆ Preheat oven to 500°.
◆ Core, but do not peel, the apple, cut into quarters, and then slice thinly. Thinly slice the Brie, leaving the rind on for a tarter taste, or removing for a smoother flavor.
◆ When the oven is ready, precook the pizza dough for two minutes. Remove the dough from the oven and top with the sliced apples, then the cheese, and finally sprinkle with the almonds.
◆ Bake for six to eight minutes, until cheese begins to brown.

MEXICAN PIZZA

MAKES ONE 12-INCH DOUBLE-CRUST PIZZA

This is really just a simple cheese pizza with a Mexican twist. The
jalapeño crust gives it a punch and lots of color. The salsa goes on
cold at the last minute.

1 batch Jalapeño-Tomato Pizza Dough
  (see page 18)
¾ cup mozzarella cheese, grated
¾ cup fresh Romano cheese, grated
½ cup Cheddar cheese, grated
½ cup bottled salsa (medium heat), chilled

◆ Preheat oven to 500°. Bake the crust for five minutes and remove from oven.
◆ Spread the mozzarella cheese around the crust, leaving ½-inch at the edge. Next spread the Romano over the mozzarella. Top that with the Cheddar cheese, but stop an inch or more from the edge. This will leave a rim of white cheese around the circle of yellow cheese. Bake for about three minutes, until cheese is melted. Right before serving, spread the salsa in the center of the pizza in a small circle.

▲ Apple and Brie Pizza.

PIZZA PAELLA

MAKES ONE 12-INCH DOUBLE-CRUST PIZZA

In this vegetarian version of classic Spanish paella, leeks replace the
fish and meat. But it retains the traditional flavoring of saffron,
garlic, and onions.

1 batch Basic Pizza Dough (see page 14)
1½ onions, chopped
2 leeks, chopped
2 tbsp olive oil
2 large cloves garlic, crushed
1 tbsp lemon zest, cut in strips
large pinch of saffron
½ tsp salt
½ tsp cayenne pepper
½ cup frozen peas, thawed
2–3 Roma tomatoes, chopped
1 2¼ oz jar sliced black olives, drained

◆ Preheat oven to 500˚.
◆ Coarsely chop the onions. Chop the leeks
into 1-inch pieces and clean thoroughly to
remove dirt. Heat the oil in a pan over
medium heat and add the onions, leeks,
garlic, lemon zest, saffron, salt, and cayenne
pepper. Sauté for five minutes or so, stirring
frequently, until onions and leeks are wilted
◆ Remove from the heat and stir in the peas
and tomatoes. Spread the mixture on the
pizza dough. Top with the drained olives.
Bake for 10 minutes.

◀ Pizza Paella.

TACO PIZZA

MAKES ONE 12-INCH DOUBLE-CRUST PIZZA

Mexican food has long been a favorite, and its ingredients go well on top of a pizza. In this vegetarian version, bean dip replaces the traditional ground beef.

1 batch Corn Bread Pizza Dough (see page 17)

1¼ cups sour cream

¼ cup mayonnaise

2 tbsp chili powder

¼ tsp cumin

½ tsp garlic powder

¼ tsp onion powder

¼ tsp salt

4–5 Roma tomatoes, chopped

8–10 scallions, chopped

1 10 oz can bean dip

¾ cup grated Cheddar cheese

◆ Preheat oven to 500˚. Cook the pizza dough for five minutes and remove from the oven. Prepare the topping.

◆ In a bowl, combine the sour cream, mayonnaise, and spices. Mix thoroughly and set aside. Chop the tomatoes and scallions and set aside.

◆ To top, first spread the bean dip over the dough using a rubber spatula. Next spread the sour cream mixture. Then spread the tomatoes and onions over the sour cream. Top with Cheddar cheese. Bake for 10 minutes.

KUNG PAO PIZZA

MAKES ONE 12-INCH DOUBLE-CRUST PIZZA

If you have a fondness for hot and spicy Chinese food, this pizza should satisfy you. This vegetarian version of a very hot dish eliminates only the meat, not the heat.

1 batch Chinese Pizza Dough (see page 20–21)
2 cups broccoli flowerets
2 cups cauliflower flowerets
2 scallions, chopped
1 small tomato, chopped
¼ cup peanuts
2 tsp sugar
2 tsp cider vinegar
2 tsp cornstarch
2 tbsp soy sauce
½ tsp crushed dried hot red pepper
6 dried whole hot red peppers
1 tbsp peanut oil

◆ Preheat oven to 500°. Bake crust for five minutes and remove from oven.

◆ Cut the broccoli and cauliflower into small flowerets, discarding stalks, and place in a bowl. Add the chopped scallions, chopped tomato and peanuts.

◆ In a separate container, add the sugar, vinegar, cornstarch, soy sauce, and crushed red pepper and stir to mix thoroughly. Pour the liquid over the vegetables, coating well. Marinate for about five minutes.

◆ To assemble the pizza, spread the marinated vegetables over the crust, adding any of the liquid not absorbed. Attractively arrange the whole red peppers on top. Sprinkle the pizza with peanut oil and bake for five minutes.

REUBEN PIZZA

MAKES ONE 12-INCH DOUBLE-CRUST PIZZA

You don't miss the corned beef at all in this vegetarian-pizza
version of a Reuben sandwich. A little chili powder gives it
color and spice.

1 batch Rye Bread Pizza Dough
  (see page 22–23)
1 cup mayonnaise
¼ cup chili sauce
1 8 oz can sauerkraut
½ tsp caraway seeds (optional)
1 small onion
1¼ cups Swiss cheese, grated
½ tsp mild chili powder

◆ Preheat oven to 500°.
◆ In a bowl, mix mayonnaise and chili
sauce together. Spread the mixture over the
pizza dough, leaving a ½-inch edge. Drain
the sauerkraut and squeeze to eliminate as
much moisture as possible. Spread the
sauerkraut over the sauce. If using caraway
seeds, spread them over the sauerkraut.
Slice the onion and separate into rings.
Place the rings on the sauerkraut. Top with
the grated Swiss cheese. Sprinkle ½
teaspoon of mild chili powder over the
pizza. Bake for 10 minutes.

PIZZA STROGANOFF

MAKES ONE 12-INCH DOUBLE-CRUST PIZZA

Meatless stroganoff made with mushrooms, broccoli, and onions
is a hearty topping for a pizza. Sour cream and Monterey Jack
make a rich sauce, and sunflower seeds add a little crunch.

1 batch Whole Wheat Pizza Dough
  (see page 16)
1 tbsp butter
1½ onions, chopped
2 cups chopped mushrooms
1 tsp basil
1tsp salt
juice of 1 lemon
1 cup sour cream
1 cup shredded Monterey Jack
3 cups broccoli flowerets
2 tbsp sunflower seeds

◆ Preheat the oven to 500°.
◆ Melt the butter in a pan and sauté the
chopped onions, mushrooms, basil, and salt
over medium heat until vegetables are soft.
Remove from the heat and add the lemon
juice, sour cream, and cheese. Stir to blend.
◆ Wash and drain the broccoli and separate
it into small flowerets. To assemble the
pizza, spread the broccoli over the pizza
dough. Sprinkle the sunflower seeds over
the broccoli. Top with the sour cream
mixture. Bake for 10 minutes.

▲ Reuben Pizza.

BREAKFAST PIZZA

This filling entrée is like omelet and toast all in one. Serve with
hot coffee and fresh fruit for a delicious brunch for six.

1 batch Basic or Whole Wheat Pizza Dough
   (see page 16)
1½ tsp butter
small onion, diced
½ cup diced mushroom
6 eggs
¼ tsp salt
⅓ cup half and half
¾ cup grated Cheddar cheese

◆ Preheat oven to 500°.

◆ Spread the dough in a greased pan
9 x 13 x 2-inches. Prick the bottom in a
few places with a toothpick or fork. Bake
for five minutes.

◆ Melt the butter and sauté the onions for
about three minutes, until they begin to
turn opaque. Add the mushrooms and
sauté for three minutes more. Remove from
the heat.

◆ In a bowl, beat the eggs well, using a
fork. Add the salt and half and half and
beat again.

◆ Lower the oven temperature to 450°.

◆ In the bottom of the prebaked crust,
spread the Cheddar cheese. Pour the egg
mixture over that and bake for 25 minutes.

BASIL AND PINE NUT PIZZA

Pine nuts, also known as piñon nuts or pignoi, come from the
cones of certain pine trees. An ingredient in pesto sauce, they
naturally go well with fresh basil. This is another pizza that can be
assembled more quickly than it can be eaten.

1 Basic Pizza Dough (see page 14)
handful fresh basil
¼ cup pine nuts
⅔ cup feta cheese, crumbled

◆ Preheat oven to 500°.

◆ Wash and dry the basil and chop it into
bite-sized pieces. Spread the basil over the
pizza dough, leaving a ½-inch edge. Spread
the pine nuts over the basil. Top with the
crumbled feta cheese. Bake for five to eight
minutes.

◄ Breakfast
Pizza.

PIZZAS
WITH INSPIRED
CRUSTS

▚▚▚▚▚

THREE MUSHROOMS CALZONE

MAKES FOUR CALZONES

Any combination of mushrooms goes well in this folded pizza,
which is like a hearty sandwich. Try to use more than one variety
each time for a more exciting flavor.

1 batch Whole Wheat Pizza Dough (see
    page 16)
¼ cup olive oil
8 oz portabella mushrooms, chopped
4 oz shiitake mushrooms, chopped
4 oz enoki mushrooms
2 tsp minced garlic
2 tsp dried sage
2 tsp dried parsley
4 oz grated Swiss cheese
8 oz grated fontina cheese

◆ Preheat oven to 500°.
◆ Divide dough into four balls. Roll each
one into a flat circle about 6-inches in
diameter. Brush with olive oil. Chop the
portabella and shiitake mushrooms into
small pieces.
◆ On one half of each circle of dough,
place 2 ounces of portabella mushrooms
(about 2 tablespoons), ½ ounce of enoki
mushrooms (a clump about ½ inch in
diameter) and 1 ounce (about 1 tablespoon)
of shiitake mushrooms. Add ½ teaspoon
minced garlic. Sprinkle with ½ teaspoon
each of sage and parsley. Top with 2 ounces
fontina and 1 ounce Swiss cheese.
◆ Fold the dough in half until the edges
meet and press slightly to seal. Brush with
olive oil and poke a few holes in the top
with a toothpick or fork.
◆ Bake on a greased baking sheet for 15
minutes.

INDIVIDUAL PESTO PIZZAS

MAKES FOUR 6-INCH PIZZAS

Homemade pesto is so good it's worth growing a crop of basil in your garden in order to have easy access. These pizzas make great appetizers, but are also good as the main course for lunch.

4 pieces of pita bread (6-inch diameter)
1 small red onion, thinly sliced
1 small Roma tomato, thinly sliced
4 oz feta cheese, crumbled

Pesto sauce:
½ cup fresh basil leaves, no stems
1 heaping tablespoon pine nuts
1 large clove garlic, minced
¼ cup extra-virgin olive oil
¼ cup Parmesan cheese

◆ First make the pesto sauce. Put the basil, pine nuts, garlic, olive oil, and Parmesan cheese in a blender or food processor and mix until thoroughly blended. Make ahead of time and refrigerate if you wish.

◆ To make the pizza, toast the pita bread. Then top each piece with 1 tablespoon of pesto sauce, a slice of onion, a slice of tomato, and finally, an ounce of feta cheese.

◄ Individual pesto pizzas.

MINI COCKTAIL PIZZAS

MAKES EIGHT MINI PIZZAS

Use English muffins as the recipe suggests, or a prebaked crust
cut into small circles. These simple *hors d'oeuvres* are pretty to look
at as well as tasty to eat.

8 English muffin halves

½ cup Pizza Sauce (see page 28)

4 oz shredded Swiss cheese

1 ripe medium tomato

2 tsp olive oil

4 tsp fresh parsley, minced

◆ Lightly toast the muffin halves. Then spread 1 tablespoon of pizza sauce on each muffin half. Top with ½ ounce Swiss cheese. Broil in a toaster oven for about five minutes, or until cheese is bubbly and begins to turn brown. Slice the tomato in thin, perfect rounds. Top each broiled muffin with one tomato slice. Brush with a little olive oil and sprinkle with about ½ teaspoon of parsley. Serve immediately.

SPINACH AND WALNUT
APPETIZER PIZZAS

MAKES 12 APPETIZER PIZZAS

Walnut oil, which can be purchased in health food stores, makes
an unusual vinaigrette for this appetizer pizza. Choose a good-
quality Gorgonzola for the tangy, creamy topping.

12 English muffin halves

½ cup walnut oil

1 cup walnut halves, broken

2 tbsp red wine vinegar

½ tsp salt

2 scallions, finely chopped

4 oz fresh spinach, stems removed

6 oz Gorgonzola cheese

◆ Pour the oil over the walnuts and marinate for about 15 minutes. Strain the walnuts and set aside. Mix the vinegar, salt, and finely chopped scallions into the oil.

◆ Toast the muffins to a light brown. Wash the spinach and remove the stems. Pat dry and place about three leaves on each of the toasted muffins. Top with a scant tablespoon of the dressing, 1 tablespoon of walnuts, and top with about ½ ounce of cheese. Broil for about three minutes until cheese begins to melt.

◄ Mini cocktail
pizzas.

TABBOULEH APPETIZER PIZZAS

MAKES 8 PITA BREAD PIZZAS

This recipe combines tabbouleh, the bulgur salad with a hint of mint, and feta cheese. Because good tabbouleh needs to chill in the refrigerator, make it ahead of time. When it's time to eat, assemble and bake the appetizers in just a few minutes.

8 pita breads (6-inch diameter)
⅔ cup bulgur
¾ cup boiling water
¼ cup finely chopped fresh mint (start with 1
   cup loosely packed leaves)
1 cup finely chopped parsley
2 scallions, finely chopped

¼ cup olive oil
juice of 1 lemon
½ tsp salt
2 Roma tomatoes, diced
½ cup sliced almonds
8 oz crumbled feta cheese

◆ To make the tabbouleh, cover the bulgur with boiling water and set aside for 30 minutes. The water should be completely absorbed. When the bulgur is ready, add the fresh mint, parsley, and scallions. Stir in the olive oil, lemon juice, and salt. Finely dice the tomatoes and gently mix into the tabbouleh. Store in the refrigerator until ready to use.

◆ To make the pizzas, lightly toast the pita bread. Then spread 1 tablespoon of sliced almonds on each piece. Spread approximately ½ cup of tabbouleh over the nuts on each pita. Top with 1 ounce of feta cheese. Place under hot broiler for two or three minutes until feta just begins to melt.

PIZZA CUPS

MAKES 12 PIZZA CUPS

Baking miniature pizzas in muffin tins makes an interesting variation for an *hors d'oeuvre*. This recipe calls for a topping of onions and mushrooms, but any favorite vegetable could be used.

3⅓ cups Bisquick
2 tbsp olive oil
½ cup milk
1 small onion, chopped
¾ cup mushrooms, sliced
6 tbsp Pizza Sauce (see page 28)
½ cup grated mozzarella cheese

◆ Preheat oven to 450°.

◆ In a bowl, mix 2 cups of the Bisquick with the oil and the milk. When well combined, slowly add the remaining Bisquick, kneading until a stiff dough forms. Using a rolling pin or the palm of your hand, flatten the dough until it is about ½-inch thick. Using a glass with a 2½-3 inch diameter, cut 12 circles in the dough. Rotate each circle between your fingers, pressing it until it is ⅛-inch thick and about 4 inches in diameter. Place one circle in each cup of a lightly oiled, non-stick muffin tin and push it down so that it forms a cup. (Muffin tin should make muffins approximately 3 inches in diameter.)

◆ Divide the onions and mushrooms equally between the 12 cups. Top with approximately 1½ teaspoons of pizza sauce and 1½ tablespoons of cheese. Bake for 15 minutes until the edges brown and cheese melts.

◄ Tabbouleh appetizer pizzas

CHEESE AND GUACAMOLE
PIZZA WEDGES

MAKES 24 APPETIZER WEDGES

Tortillas baked with cheese are popular pizzas in the Southwest. Mexican restaurants in Arizona serve them on giant tortillas, 12 or more inches in diameter. But unless you make your own, that size is not readily available. This recipe uses 8-inch tortillas, which are easy to find, and are a good size for appetizers.

6 flour tortillas (8-inch diameter)

1 ripe avocado, mashed

¾ cup bottled salsa

1½ cups grated Cheddar cheese

1 large clove garlic, minced

2 tbsp bottled pickled jalapeño peppers, chopped

2 tsp juice from pickled jalapeños

½ tsp salt

◆ To make the guacamole, mash the avocado with a fork. Add the minced (or pressed) garlic and the chopped bottled jalapeño peppers, along with 2 teaspoons liquid from the bottle. Stir in the salt. Store in the refrigerator until ready to serve.

◆ To make the pizzas, lightly toast the tortillas (easiest in a toaster oven). Remove from the oven and top each tortilla with 2 tablespoons of salsa, then ¼ cup of the grated Cheddar cheese. Broil for about three minutes, until cheese melts. To serve, cut each tortilla into quarters. Top each quarter with a teaspoon of guacamole.

HUMMUS AND VEGETABLE PIZZA

MAKES 12 APPETIZER-SIZED PIZZAS

Hummus is a mixture of puréed garbanzo beans and tahini –
ground sesame seed butter – and is usually served as a dip for pita
bread or vegetables. It goes just as well on top of a pizza. Top with
sliced vegetables and a pecan half.

12 English muffin halves

1½ cups garbanzo beans

¼ cup tahini

juice of 1 lemon

2 cloves garlic

2 tbsp sesame seeds

1 tsp coriander

1 tsp cumin

1 small cucumber, peeled and thinly sliced

2 Roma tomatoes, thinly sliced

12 pecan halves

◆ To make the hummus, purée the
garbanzo beans in a food processor. Add
the tahini, lemon juice, garlic cloves, and
purée until mixed well.

◆ In a separate bowl, stir together the
sesame seeds, coriander, and cumin. Peel
and thinly slice the cucumber and tomatoes
into rounds.

◆ To assemble, lightly toast the muffins.
Then spread a heaped tablespoon of the
hummus on each muffin half. Top with
about five cucumber rounds, slightly
overlapped to look like petals. Place a slice
of tomato in the center. Sprinkle on a half
teaspoon of the sesame seed mixture and
top with a pecan half. Bake in a toaster
oven at 375° for about five minutes.

LEEK AU GRATIN CALZONE

These mild vegetables are well complemented by the sharp,
somewhat nutty taste of the Gruyère. Leeks are often sandy at the
root so make sure you wash them thoroughly.

1 batch Whole Wheat Pizza Dough (see
page 16)

4 tbsp butter

4 tbsp whole wheat flour

½ cup milk

1 egg yolk

½ cup grated Gruyère cheese

1 large leek

½ tsp salt

¼ tsp pepper

¼ cup olive oil

◆ Preheat oven to 500˚.

◆ Melt the butter in a pan and add the flour, stirring to make a roux. Cook for two to three minutes and slowly add the milk. Stir until the roux thickens and bubbles. Remove from the heat and stir in the egg yolk. Add the grated cheese.

◆ Remove the root and then chop the leek into ½-inch pieces. Wash thoroughly to remove any dirt and drain in a colander. Pat dry and then stir into the cheese mixture.

Stir in the salt and pepper.

◆ Divide the dough into four balls. Roll each one into a flat circle about six inches in diameter. Brush with olive oil.

◆ Divide the leek mixture between the four dough circles, placing it on one half of the circle only. Fold the dough in half until the edges meet and press slightly to seal. Brush with olive oil and poke a few holes in the top with a toothpick. Bake on greased baking sheet for 15 minutes.

◄ Leek au Gratin Calzone.

DESSERT PIZZAS

DESSERT FRUIT PIZZA

This is the most beautiful dessert pizza you can serve and is always a hit. You can vary the fruit depending on what's in season and what you like. Follow the instructions below to arrange the fruit, or create your own designs.

1 batch Dessert Pizza Crust (see page 24)

8 oz cream cheese

8 oz frozen whipped cream topping

2 kiwi fruit

5 large strawberries

1 11-oz can mandarin oranges, drained

◈ Allow the cream cheese to soften to room temperature. Then mix the whipped cream topping and cream cheese together until smooth using an electric mixer. Spread the mixture over the baked and cooled dessert pizza crust. Put it in the refrigerator while you prepare the fruit.

◈ Gently peel the two kiwis and slice one kiwi into thin rounds. Slice the second kiwi into thin rounds and then cut those in half. You will have two shapes of kiwis: circles and half circles.

◈ Wash and slice off the tops of the strawberries. Slice them so that the pieces are more or less round. Separate the slices into large and small sizes (larger circles from the center of the berry, smaller from the ends.

◈ To top the pizza, begin with the outer ring, using one orange segment, then one half-circle kiwi. The oranges should point in toward the centre; the diameters of the kiwi should face the orange. Nestle the fruit close together. Proceed along the rim alternating the kiwi and orange segments. For the second ring, use a full-circle kiwi and a large strawberry circle. For the third ring, use orange segments and smaller strawberry circles. End with a full-circle kiwi slice for the center.

◈ Refrigerate and serve chilled.

CHOCOLATE PIZZA CRISP

MAKES ONE REGULAR 12-INCH PIZZA

This pizza is a variation of rice crispie treats. Peanuts, coconut, M&Ms®, and chocolate chips have been added to make this a chocolate lover's delight.

12 oz package semi-sweet chocolate chips
3 oz butter
2 cups miniature marshmallows
1–2 tbsp milk
1 cup crisp rice cereal
½ cup shredded coconut
½ cup miniature M&Ms®
½ cup unsalted dry roasted peanuts

◆ In the top of a double boiler, melt the chocolate chips, butter, and marshmallows. When completely blended, remove from the heat and add a tablespoon or two of milk to attain a creamy mixture. Add the rice cereal and blend as thoroughly as possible. Mix in the coconut, M&Ms®, and peanuts. Spray a 12-inch pizza pan with cooking spray. Spread the chocolate mixture into the pan, pressing it down firmly. Refrigerate for one hour or more, until firm.

PINEAPPLE FLUFF PIZZA

MAKES ONE REGULAR 12-INCH PIZZA

Instant pudding gives this pizza topping the perfect consistency and cuts the sweetness of the pineapple.

1 batch Gingerbread Crust (see page 24)
1 8-oz can pineapple rings, drained with ¼
    cup juice reserved
8 oz cream cheese, softened
¼ cup orange juice
1 ¾-oz box of instant vanilla pudding
½ tsp nutmeg
1 cup mandarin oranges, drained for garnish
    (optional)

◆ Drain the pineapple rings and reserve the juice. Set aside one pineapple ring for garnish and chop the rest into small pieces.
◆ With an electric mixer, beat the cream cheese and orange juice together. Then add the instant pudding and nutmeg. Finally, add the chopped pineapples and juice. Put in the refrigerator for 15 minutes to gel.
◆ Using a spatula, spread the pineapple fluff over the cooled gingerbread crust. Place a pineapple circle in the center for garnish. Surround the pineapple with a ring of mandarin oranges, if desired.

◄ Chocolate
Pizza Crisp.

PIZZA AMBROSIA

Ambrosia is usually a mixture of winter fruits. This recipe adds
nuts and a sweet sauce to make a fruity, healthy dessert pizza.
Make the sauce ahead of time, if possible, because it thickens as it
sits in the refrigerator.

1 Dessert Pizza Crust (see page 24)
1 egg
1 tbsp butter
1 tsp sugar
¼ cup orange juice
juice of 1 lemon (about 2 tbsp)
¼ cup heavy cream
2 oz cream cheese
1 apple, chopped
1 11-oz can mandarin oranges, drained
2 bananas, sliced
1 cup pitted dates, chopped
½ cup pecan halves
3 tbsp sweetened coconut

◈ To make the dressing, put the slightly
beaten egg, butter, and sugar in the top of
a double boiler and heat, stirring
frequently, until cooked and thickened and
smooth, about 15 minutes. Remove from
the heat and add the orange and lemon
juices and refrigerate. When mixture has
cooled, pour into a bowl and, using an
electric mixer on high, slowly add the
cream and cream cheese. Beat until smooth
and creamy. If there is time, refrigerate for
an hour to thicken before using.

◈ Seed, but don't peel the apple and
coarsely chop. Mix in a bowl with the
drained mandarin oranges, sliced bananas,
chopped dates, and pecans. Pour enough
sauce over the fruit to cover but not
saturate it. You may have dressing left over.

◈ Spread the fruit mixture over the baked,
cooled crust. Sprinkle the coconut over the
top. Serve immediately, or refrigerate for
later use.

CHOCOLATE BANANA PIZZA

MAKES ONE REGULAR 12-INCH PIZZA

The banana split inspired this dessert pizza, a combination of chocolate and bananas. A cream cheese, yogurt, and honey sauce replaces the ice cream.

1 Chocolate Dessert Crust (see page 23)
4 oz cream cheese
½ cup plain yogurt
1½ tsp honey
3 large or 4 medium bananas, sliced
2 oz semi-sweet chocolate, shaved or grated

◈ Soften the cream cheese to room temperature and then beat in the yogurt and honey. Slice the bananas into rounds about ¼–½ inch thick and place on the crust in a single layer. Pour the yogurt and cream cheese mixture over the bananas. Top with chocolate. Refrigerate until ready to serve.

◁ Chocolate banana pizza.

121

MINTED MELON PIZZA

MAKES ONE REGULAR 12-INCH PIZZA

The sauce for this pizza has the cool flavor of mint that goes so well with berries and melon. The sauce is very sweet, and so is the crust, so don't drown the fruit.

1 Chocolate Dessert Crust, baked and cooled (see page 23)
¼ cup sugar
½ cup water
4 or 5 fresh mint leaves
1 large ripe cantaloupe, chopped
1 cup fresh blueberries
mint leaves for garnish

◆ In a pan, mix the sugar, water, and mint leaves. Bring to a boil and simmer for five minutes, reducing liquid to about ¼ cup. Remove and discard the mint leaves and cool the sugar water in the refrigerator.

◆ Cut the cantalope in half, remove the seeds, and chop into small squares. Wash and sort the blueberries, removing stems and bad berries.

◆ To assemble, spread the melon over the crust. Sprinkle the blueberries on top. Pour the sugar water over the fruit (but do not drawn the fruit – you may not need to use all the sugar water). Garnish with mint leaves.

APPLE CRISP PIZZA

Apples paired with gingerbread are a delicious combination. Use
any type of good, firm apple for this recipe. It can be served by
itself or, like a pie, with ice cream or whipped cream.

1 Gingerbread Crust, unbaked (see
   page 24)
2 or 3 large apples such as Red Delicious,
   peeled and sliced
1 cup white flour
½ cup packed dark brown sugar
1 tsp cinnamon
1 tsp ginger
½ tsp mace
½ cup butter
½ cup walnut pieces

◆ Preheat oven to 350°.
◆ Peel the apples and remove the stem and seeds. Slice them thinly.
◆ To make the topping, mix flour, brown sugar, cinnamon, ginger, and mace together in a bowl and stir to blend. Using two knives, cut in the butter until crumbly. Mix in the walnut pieces.
◆ To assemble the pizza, arrange the apple slices on the gingerbread dough. Spread the topping over the apples. Bake for 15 minutes at 350°.

COOKIE PIZZA

A giant chocolate chip cookie is what this pizza really is. Because
it's so rich, it should be served in small pieces.

½ cup butter, softened to room temperature
   (1 stick)
½ cup packed brown sugar
¼ cup white sugar
½ tsp baking soda
1 egg
1 tsp vanilla
1¼ cups flour
6 oz semi-sweet chocolate chips
¾ cup walnut pieces

◆ Preheat oven to 350°.
◆ Cream the softened butter and sugars together. Mix in baking soda, egg, and vanilla. Add the flour and mix thoroughly. Add the chocolate chips and walnuts. For easier roll-out, put the dough in the refrigerator for 15 to 30 minutes to stiffen. Spread the dough as evenly as possible on a greased 12-inch pizza pan. Bake for 20 minutes at 350°. Allow to cool for about 15 minutes before cutting.

▲ Apple Crisp Pizza.

PEARS IN PORT WINE PIZZA

Marinate the pears ahead of time so that they turn a nice deep purple, and save the port marinade for an after-dinner drink! It is deliciously flavored by the fruit and spices.

1 batch Dessert Pizza Crust (see page 24)
4 ripe pears
½ cup raisins
1 stick cinnamon
8 whole allspice berries
1 bottle port wine
whipped cream

◆ Select ripe pears that are no longer crisp because they absorb the wine more easily. Peel and seed them and cut into slices about ¼-inch thick. Put them in a glass jar with the raisins, cinnamon, and allspice. Add the wine, which should completely cover the fruit. Cover the jar and refrigerate overnight or for up to three days.
◆ To assemble, drain the fruit, reserving the port. Discard the cinnamon stick. Spread the fruit on the baked, cooled crust in an even layer, leaving a ¼-inch edge. Pour ¼ cup of the port over the fruit. Decorate the pizza with a ring of whipped cream around the outer edge of the fruit, and another in the center.

PEACH AND RASPBERRY PIZZA

This dessert pizza offers a nice contrast between the tart berries and the sweet crust. It is a beautiful dessert to serve during the summer when fruit is at its peak of ripeness.

1 Dessert Pizza Crust (see page 24)
1½ cups raspberries
1 tbsp Grand Marnier liqueur
2 ripe peaches, sliced

◆ Purée the raspberries in a food processor and chop. Pour into a bowl, add the Grand Marnier, and stir. Cut the peaches in half and remove the pits. Cut each half in half again and slice thinly. Arrange the slices on the cooked, cooled crust so that they overlap slightly. Pour the raspberry mixture over the peaches and serve.

◄ Pears in port wine pizza.

INDEX